Votes and More for Women: Suffrage and After in Connecticut

The *Women & History* series:

- *Beautiful Merchandise: Prostitution in China 1860 - 1936,* by Sue Gronewold
- *The Empire of the Mother: American Writing about Domesticity 1830 - 1860,* by Mary P. Ryan
- *Women, Family, and Community in Colonial America: Two Perspectives,* by Alison Duncan Hirsch and Linda Speth, with an Introduction by Carol Berkin
- *Votes and More for Women: Suffrage and After in Connecticut,* by Carole Nichols, with a Foreword by Lois Banner

Forthcoming:

- *A New Song: Celibate Women in the First Three Christian Centuries,* by JoAnn McNamara
- *"Dames Employées": The Feminization of Postal Work in Nineteenth-Century France,* by Susan Bachrach
- *Women in the Enlightenment,* by Margaret Hunt, Margaret Jacob, Phyllis Mack, and Ruth Perry, with a Foreword by Ruth Graham

Votes and More for Women: Suffrage and After in Connecticut

Carole Nichols

Copublished by
The Institute for Research in History and The Haworth Press, Inc.

Votes and More for Women: Suffrage and After in Connecticut has also been published as *Women & History,* Number 5, Spring 1983.

Copyright © 1983 by The Haworth Press, Inc. All rights reserved. Copies of chapters in this work may be reproduced noncommercially for the purpose of educational or scientific advancement. Otherwise, no part of this work may be reproduced or utilized in any form or by any means, electronic or mechanical, including photocopying, microfilm, and recording, or by any information storage and retrieval system, without permission in writing from the publisher. Printed in the United States of America.

The Haworth Press, Inc., 28 East 22 Street, New York, NY 10010

Library of Congress Cataloging in Publication Data

Nichols, Carole.
    Votes and more for women.

        "Also . . . published as Women & history, number 5, spring 1983"—T.p. verso.
        Bibliography: p.
        Includes index.
        1. Women—Suffrage—Connecticut—History. 2. Feminism—Connecticut—History.
I. Title.
JK1911.C8N52   1983   324.6'23'09746   83-8405
ISBN 0-86656-192-7

EDITOR: ELEANOR S. RIEMER

ASSOCIATE EDITOR: ALICE MILLER

CONTRIBUTING EDITOR: LOIS BANNER

BOARD OF ADVISORS

PHYLLIS ANDORS, *Wagner College*
LOIS BANNER, *George Washington University*
RENATE BRIDENTHAL, *Brooklyn College, City University of New York**
SANDI COOPER, *College of Staten Island, City University of New York**
LEONORE DAVIDOFF, *University of Essex, England*
ELIZABETH FOX-GENOVESE, *State University of New York, Binghamton*
BARBARA HARRIS, *Pace University**
DOROTHY HELLY, *Hunter College, City University of New York**
BARBARA S. KANNER, *Occidental College*
ALICE KESSLER-HARRIS, *Hofstra University*
GERDA LERNER, *University of Wisconsin*
KATHLEEN McCRONE, *University of Windsor, Canada*
JOANN McNAMARA, *Hunter College, City University of New York**
MARY BETH NORTON, *Cornell University*
SARAH POMEROY, *Hunter College, City University of New York**
ANNE FIROR SCOTT, *Duke University*
JOAN SCOTT, *Brown University*
CARROLL SMITH-ROSENBERG, *University of Pennsylvania*
ROSALYN TERBORG-PENN, *Morgan State University*
MARCIA WRIGHT, *Columbia University**

*A Fellow of the Institute for Research in History

About the Author

Carole Nichols is currently Coordinator of the Women's History Program at Sarah Lawrence College, where she earned an M.A. in Women's History in 1979. She and Joyce Pendery recently completed a two-year oral history project, "The Political Activities of the First Generation of Fully Enfranchised Connecticut Women," funded by the Connecticut Humanities Council under the auspices of the University of Connecticut at Storrs.

Votes and More for Women: Suffrage and After in Connecticut

Women & History
Number 5

CONTENTS

Foreword *Lois W. Banner*	ix
Introduction	1
Chapter I: The Emergence of the Women's Movement in Connecticut	5
Chapter II: Winning the Vote: The Final Years	23
Chapter III: The Responsibility of Victory	37
Notes	52
Bibliography	65
Appendix	70
Index	87

Foreword

During a decade or more of vigorous scholarship in women's history, the suffrage movement has been curiously overlooked. Despite its centrality to women's organizational activity, the century-long attempt to secure the vote for women awaits its modern chroniclers. The reasons for this oversight are several. The publication of a number of impressive works on the subject in the late 1950s and 1960s seemed to preempt the necessity for further investigation.[1] More important, the prevailing view of earlier historians that suffrage was all there was to women's history provoked newly-emerging historians of women and motivated them to probe the depths of women's experience in all areas of life. Suffrage was relegated to secondary consideration. Yet the movement for the vote, more than any other, linked women around a common cause and brought together the disparate meanings of their social involvements. It is high time for a reinterpretation of suffrage as an integrative experience in the light of the impressive scholarship on women during recent years.

Focusing on the state of Connecticut, Carole Nichols has written a significant chapter in the final suffrage narrative. Most important, her conclusions suggest a version somewhat different from the current conception. Attending to the state rather than the national level, Nichols finds a unified movement of women—not only during the Progressive era of suffrage achievement but also during the 1920s, when women's organizations are generally presumed to have fallen into a self-defeating factionalism which doomed further reform endeavor. There was no split in Connecticut, for example, between the League of Women Voters and the Woman's Party. Both remained largely autonomous from the national organization, and together they pursued a vigorous program, including demands for

---

[1] See Eleanor Flexner, *Century of Struggle: The Woman's Rights Movement in the United States* (New York, 1959); Aileen S. Kraditor, *The Ideas of the Woman Suffrage Movement, 1890-1920* (New York, 1965); William L. O'Neill, *Everyone Was Brave: The Rise and Fall of Feminism in America* (New York, 1969).

juvenile courts, maternity and health care, birth control, and women's rights—both before and after the war. If anything, the conservative Republican Party which controlled the state government confounded women's attempts at reform—both in the Progressive era and in the 1920s. Nichols's research raises interesting questions about the locus of authority within American women's voluntary organizations, about the generational continuity and discontinuity among groups of American women, about the whole interpretation of the 1920s as the "roaring twenties," dominated by sex and speakeasies and the rejection of the Progressive crusade for social justice. Along with recent works by Susan Becker and Lois Scharf, Nichols brings the politics of women's organizations into closer perspective and suggests that the feminism of the 1910s endured into the 1920s in ways historians have not paid full attention to.[2] And she strongly suggests that we should shift our prevailing attention from the national to the state level if we are fully to assemble the puzzle of the seeming failure of women's reform action after the passage of suffrage. There we may find that women were not in fact unintentional culprits in feminism's demise but rather victims of forces dominated by men over which they had no control.

Lois W. Banner
Professor of History
George Washington University
Washington, DC

---

[2]Susan Becker, *The Origins of the Equal Rights Amendment: American Feminism Between the Wars* (Westport, CT, 1981); Lois Scharf, *To Work and To Wed: Female Employment, Feminism, and the Great Depression* (Westport, 1980).

The Executive Board of the C.W.S.A., 1917. (Rear: left to right) Mabel C. Washburn; Emily Pierson; and Annie G. Porritt; (Front: left to right) Mary J. Rogers; Caroline Ruutz-Rees; Katharine H. Hepburn; Maud T. Hincks; unidentified; unidentified; and Katherine B. Day. Reprinted by permission of the Connecticut State Library Archives, Record Group 101.

Introduction

It is commonly assumed that woman suffrage had little impact on American politics. Indeed, in the opinion of some scholars, the early twentieth-century women's movement was a failure;[1] government remained in the hands of men and few reforms reflecting women's interests were enacted. According to this view, suffragists themselves are to blame for their "failure."[2] Historians have further questioned their commitment to reform, their willingness to identify with factory workers, their ability to organize the newly enfranchised, and even their capacity to understand the political and economic realities of American life.[3] Feminists in the post-suffrage era tend to be depicted as divided, and absorbed in ideological conflicts that caused them to lose their effectiveness.[4] In sum, we have been left with the impression that social legislation was not passed, and feminism waned, after the ratification of the Nineteenth Amendment because most American women were politically conservative or indifferent to political issues and because feminists did not exercise the power that was available to them.[5]

The analyses of most historians have been limited—and skewed—by their exclusive focus upon the national suffrage organizations and their leaders, and on the struggle to secure passage of the federal suffrage amendment. In so doing, they have failed to recognize that most feminist activity occurred on the local and state levels, and that most women emerged as political activists within the context of their own communities, driven by their concern for the welfare of their fellow citizens.

In the late nineteenth century, small groups of women organized equal-rights leagues, which convened annually to plan petition campaigns, support sympathetic candidates, and lobby at legislative sessions. Most of these efforts, conducted under the auspices of state organizations, with relatively loose ties to their national affiliates, were aimed at influencing state and local government. Similarly, in the final years of the suffrage campaign, state, not national, politics drew most feminists' attention and energies. Holding to the view that the federal amendment offered the best hope for enfranchisement, suffragists realized that they had to pressure Congressmen and Senators to vote for the amendment, and to elect pro-suffrage representatives to the state legislatures.[7]

Moreover, after the vote was won, women continued to seek passage of state legislation that would provide health care for infants and mothers, better working conditions in factories, the abolition of child labor, jury duty for women, liberal birth control laws, improved correctional facilities, and other measures benefiting women, children, and the family. Once enfranchised, of course, women were able to promote their programs as members of local and state party committees, as candidates for office, and as government officials.[8]

The examination of state and local history thus allows us to understand better and document more fully the women's movement of the late nineteenth and early twentieth centuries. Such an approach offers an appropriate and realistic ground for testing the generalizations of those historians who have written from a national perspective.

The purpose of this study is to weigh assumptions about the suffrage movement and its aftermath against the evidence and experience of women in one state—Connecticut. My findings bring into question a number of prevailing notions regarding the movement's leadership, goals, tactics, ideology, and impact, and suggest that this particuarly complex period in women's political history cannot be explained adequately by continued reliance on a national perspective. Further research on other states is necessary before final conclusions can be drawn.[9]

Even before enfranchisement was secured, the Connecticut suffragists had begun to lay the groundwork for the post-suffrage era. Understanding that enfranchisement alone was not sufficient to ensure the advancement of women in government or the enactment of social welfare legislation, they sought full participation of women in local, state, and national politics. Both before and after ratification of the Nineteenth Amendment, feminists aligned themselves with factory workers and advocated protective legislation, higher pay, shorter hours, and workers' compensation. Connecticut suffragists appear to be politically sophisticated and democratic; more importantly, their movement was not "destroyed," nor did they destroy it, during the 1920s.

While tactical differences arose before and after suffrage, the Connecticut women's movement remained cohesive. If only a portion of their agenda was accepted in the post-suffrage era, it was not for lack of trying. As this study demonstrates, the strength of the opposition, namely the conservative, pro-business Republicans who dominated state politics until the Great Depression, and not a feminist failure of will, stalled the passage of social welfare bills. The resistance to reform-minded women and their causes did not wane in the 1920s.

Feminism was inherently antagonistic to the established political order in Connecticut. The women's movement had grown because suffrage leaders endorsed causes of special interest to women—causes which were, in fact, a threat to the control of the state by conservative Republicans. These politicians, consequently, obstructed women's efforts to atttain influential positions in government and in the Republican party. The study of Connecticut underscores the conflict between male politicians who wished to keep their power and politically-minded women who wanted to extend their power to advance their causes.

The findings on Connecticut support those historians who have credited women's groups with keeping social welfare issues before the public during the 1920s when radical and even progressive ideas were suspect.[10] Connecticut suffragist Ruth McIntire Dadourian wrote in 1927 that reform-minded women were aware that the "job [was] not yet finished." According to Dadourian, former suffragists and women new to politics were "thoroughly alive to certain aspects which so far have not interested the men." She noted how women gave wide publicity to feminist and social-welfare issues "which would have been buried but for the women."[11]

Despite the obstacles, the participation of women in Connecticut politics increased during the 1920s, particularly on the local level, where women served as organization leaders, elected and appointed officials, and party workers. Many women, introduced to politics through their membership in the League of Women Voters, later became party activists and office-holders. Local leagues, moreover, had some success in their own communities as backers of town charter revision, conservation, school construction, citizenship education, and the development of recreational facilities. Women's groups were far less successful in securing passage of state legislation in the 1920s.[12]

During the upheavals of the Depression era, the Republican bosses finally lost their hold on Connecticut politics. With the backing of the popular four-term Democratic Governor Wilbur Cross, elected for the first time in 1930, the General Assembly passed a number of measures which women's groups had advocated for many years. Among these were the elimination of sweatshops and the restriction of hours of work of women and children. In 1937 women also were granted the right to sit on juries.[13]

A few women held key positions in relief agencies established to deal with problems created by the Depression. The chief administrator of the Connecticut Unemployment and Relief Commission was a woman, Eleanor H. Little of Guilford. At least two former suffragists, Ruth McIntire Dadourian and Caroline Ruutz-Rees, were New Deal officials. Other former suffragists attained influential positions in the ascendant Democratic party and the Federation of Democratic Women's Clubs (see Appendix). By the end of the decade, a woman had been elected to the office of Secretary of the State. Women's involvement in community affairs continued, and their influence in local politics expanded. During the next few decades, some of these women moved into positions of leadership in state government and within political parties.[14] In spite of the barriers which stood in the way of their advancement, women's achievements in the post-suffrage era were considerable. Perhaps even more remarkable are suffragists' lifelong struggles to make the world a better place in which to live and work.

Chapter I
The Emergence of the Women's Movement in Connecticut

Organized feminist activity in Connecticut began in 1869 with the formation of the Connecticut Woman Suffrage Association (CWSA). For the next forty years, agitation for women's rights was carried on by a few individuals, who collected signatures, proposed legislation, and spoke in favor of woman suffrage and the extension of women's property rights.[1]

Women's participation in public life expanded during this period. They established day nurseries, kindergartens, and traveling libraries; crusaded against vice; served on school boards and in a few other offices available to them; and lobbied at the state legislature. Membership in the suffrage leagues remained small, however, and feminist campaigns stirred little public interest. Meanwhile, the state government had fallen into the hands of conservative Republicans. The prospects for the advancement of women's rights and social welfare legislation diminished.[2]

Not until the end of the first decade of the twentieth century did a full-scale women's movement emerge in Connecticut. Indeed, the story of organized feminism between 1869 and 1909 makes all the more striking the great surge of activity in the following years. By 1920, Connecticut women had gained the full franchise; they had built an organization claiming thousands of members and widespread public support; and they figured among the state's most vocal and energetic reformers. These developments occurred in the face of powerful opposition from the Republican political machine that dominated the state and many local governments.

Early Feminist Activity

Pioneering efforts to win the franchise in Connecticut were made by Frances Ellen Burr, a lecturer and writer, who had attended her first women's rights convention in Cleveland in 1853. Her early attempts to form a suffrage association in her own state were unsuccessful, though she was able to secure enough petitions to bring the suffrage issue before the Connecticut House of Representatives for the first time in 1867. That bill was defeated 111 to 93; however, the vote indicated substantial support among Connecticut lawmakers. Nonetheless, Burr later wrote to Susan B. Anthony that she was "pretty much alone here in those days, on the woman suffrage question."[3]

During the last three decades of the nineteenth century, Isabella Beecher Hooker dominated the struggle for women's rights in Connecticut. Born in 1822, she was the ninth living child of celebrated minister Lyman Beecher and half-sister of Catherine Beecher and Harriet Beecher Stowe. In the early 1860s Hooker met several abolitionists and suffragists, who inspired her to act on her own belief that sexual inequities must be abolished. In 1868 she participated with Lucy Stone, Julia Ward Howe, William Lloyd Garrison, Frederick Douglas, and Paulina Wright Davis in the founding of the New England Woman Suffrage Association. The following year, she met Susan B. Anthony and Elizabeth Cady Stanton with whom she quickly developed a close association. In the fall of 1869, Isabella Beecher Hooker, along with her attorney husband John Hooker, Francis Ellen Burr, and other leading citizens, issued the call for Connecticut's first suffrage convention.[4]

The 1869 convention was a "notable assemblage of men and women," including the conservative New England suffragists and also leaders of the newly formed, New York based and more radical National Woman Suffrage Association. Among the participants were Paulina Wright Davis, Julia Ward Howe, Susan B. Anthony, Elizabeth Cady Stanton, Henry Ward Beecher, Harriet Beecher Stowe, Catherine Beecher, William Lloyd Garrison, and the Reverend Olympia Brown. Press reports were favorable. Governor and Mrs. Marshall Jewell entertained the participants, and on the morning after the meeting the group assembled at the Hookers' home, "where Boston and New York amicably broke bread and discussed the fifteenth amendment together." The convention marked the founding of the Connecticut Woman Suffrage Association (CWSA).[5]

The resolutions prepared by John Hooker for the 1869 convention called for a broad range of reforms, from political and property rights to increased educational and employment opportunities for women. The resolutions noted that the extension of women's political rights "would bring to the aid of virtuous men a new and powerful element of good, which cannot be spared, and for which there can be no substitute." The group concluded that "equality of position and rights [was] intended by the Creator as the ultimate perfection of the social state." Such arguments, like the resolutions submitted before the Connecticut General Assembly in 1867, appeared consistently in feminist literature for the entire fifty-one years of the suffrage effort in the state.[6]

A small, earnest group of Connecticut reformers kept women's rights and social welfare issues alive in the final decades of the nineteenth century. Lectures, debates, and fairs were sponsored by equal rights clubs. A dramatic stand on the suffrage question was taken in the 1870s by Julia and Abby Smith, the "Maids of Glastonbury," who "resisted the collection of their taxes on the ground that they had no voice in the levy." When the women refused to back down, the town seized and sold their personal property and livestock to collect the taxes.[7]

Throughout the period, suffrage bills were presented regularly in the state legislature. Women prepared petitions and spoke for their cause at legislative hearings. Though they reported only "a melancholy record of defeats," they were granted the right to vote for school officials in 1893 and on issues related to schools and public libraries in 1909. As suffragist Annie Porritt noted, however, the 1909 law was meaningless because the state never put it into operation.[8]

In his anlysis of the woman suffrage struggle, Carl Degler concluded that most women were indifferent to the suffrage issue, and that in states where women could vote before 1920 they often did not exercise their right to do so. In these states, claimed Degler, "nothing much changed, one way or another." Consequently, he argued, the resistance by politicians waned in the later years of the movement.[9]

The history of woman suffrage in Connecticut does not support Degler's theory. Resistance to enfranchisement by politicians in power actually increased as evidence mounted that suffrage could weaken the boss system. Moreover, the decline of female participation in school elections was more than likely owing to the fact that in the 1890s party leaders generally controlled the selection of candidates and the outcome of these elections. "Women soon learned that their votes amounted to but little," explained suffragist Elizabeth Bacon in her account for the *History of Woman Suffrage*. Connecticut towns had a system of minority representation on school boards (whereby a certain number of seats were allotted to both political parties), and often the parties nominated only the exact number of candidates to be elected. Political abuses were common and charges of vote buying in local and state elections were frequent. Finally, women found that school board nominations were often used to pay political debts.[10]

Barriers to the effective use of the ballot by women marked not only this early period of limited suffrage, but also were apparent throughout the decades of this study. Connecticut politicians—both before and after ratification of the Nineteenth Amendment—obstructed the advancement of women in local and state politics by refusing to admit reform-minded women to the inner circles of party decision-making or to nominate them for office. That women did have some effect at the polls in even a few instances may explain why the politicians in the 1890s tried (unsuccessfully) to repeal the school suffrage law of 1893.[11]

An example of occasional successes by women occurred in Willimantic in 1895, when members of the local equal rights club organized a campaign to unseat a powerful member of the school board and to consolidate school districts. Women turned out to vote in such large numbers that the men reportedly put up a ladder to the voting hall and scrambled in ahead of the women using the stairway. The voter turnout by women increased almost 500 percent (from approximately 200 to 975 voters), and the women were victorious.[12]

Although they happened infrequently, these efforts to affect the outcome of school elections were reported in suffrage documents and newspapers throughout the period. In 1918, for example, suffragist Annie Porritt ran for the Hartford Board of Education. Porritt was a member of the National Woman's Party (NWP) and the Connecticut Woman Suffrage Association. Fellow suffragist Josephine Bennett wrote about Porritt's election to Mabel Vernon at NWP headquarters:

> Have you heard that Mrs. Porritt, who has been swatting the Democratic Party for years in Connecticut through the press with her usual and emphatic directness was nominated by the Democrats on the Board of Education and elected with the whole Democratic ticket? She ran ahead of the ticket, probably due to the woman's vote, which, though very light, was unquestionably nearly all in her favor. How we do antagonize the politicians![13]

Such cases suggest that full citizenship for women was indeed a threat to the political status quo and explain, at least in part, why opposition to woman suffrage intensified. Significantly, the legislature amended the school suffrage law in 1897 in order to make registration more complicated. Movement chronicler Elizabeth Bacon reported that women "believed that this change was effected to make the process of becoming a voter more disagreeable."[14]

This period was not without progress, however. Bacon also noted that, by the turn of the century, women had been elected and appointed to state and local offices, serving as school trustees, school visitors, public librarians, police matrons, notaries public, and assistant town clerks. Women were admitted to the practice of law in 1882 and, by the end of the century, a few women had attended Wesleyan University, Hartford Theological Seminary, Yale University graduate school, and Connecticut Agricultural College (now the University of Connecticut at Storrs).[15]

Moreover, in the decades following the formation of the CWSA, other legislation advantageous to women was enacted, including the strengthening of the married women's property statutes, the raising of the age of consent, and equal guardianship of children. Social-welfare legislation backed by women included prohibiting the sale of tobacco to boys under sixteen; requiring businesses to provide women and girl employees with seats when they were not performing job-related tasks; the teaching of "scientific temperance" in public schools; and compelling cities of twenty thousand or more to have police matrons. An act in 1887 established a ten-hour day for women and children under sixteen. In 1895, the General Assembly outlawed the employment of children under fourteen in factories. In 1909, factory inspection laws were strengthened.[16]

Such measures were supported by the CWSA, though its role in securing legislation is not clear. According to CWSA records, the organization publicized issues, collected signatures, and presented petitions at biennial sessions of the legislature. It is doubtful that the CWSA had much influence in legislative matters. Nonetheless, its members had close ties with some powerful politicians who were sympathetic to women's causes. These supporters were commended by the CWSA secretary Elizabeth Bacon in her 1902 article for the *History of Woman Suffrage,* and they probably deserve much of the credit for the few feminist victories of the period.[17]

Until the second decade of the twentieth century, the women's movement in Connecticut was hardly a movement at all. The CWSA, dominated by Isabella Beecher Hooker for more than thirty years, remained small and did not attract energetic young leaders. As late as 1906 the state had only three suffrage clubs, and the CWSA reported only fifty members. At the annual convention that year, the nine delegates unseated the aging Isabella Beecher Hooker (who had not attended a meeting for two years) and replaced her with long-time secretary Elizabeth Bacon. The delegate from the Long Ridge Suffrage Club gave a discouraging report to the convention and suggested that the success of her club's summer fair owed "more to the ice cream and swings for young people . . . than to any devotion to the principles of Woman Suffrage."[18]

Although only a few were suffrage activists, women became increasingly involved in community affairs during the late nineteenth and early twentieth centuries. A few were prominent supporters of progressive causes, and from this group emerged a new generation of suffragists who built a strong organization and led the feminist struggle in the state after 1909 (see Appendix).

Connecticut in the Progressive Era

In Connecticut, the late nineteenth and early twentieth centuries were characterized by the dramatic growth of industry, a large influx of foreign immigrants, and rapid urbanization. By 1910, the foreign born constituted about one-third of the state's population. By 1920, two-thirds of its people were either foreign born or first-generation Americans.[19] These changes increased the need for social-welfare programs, and women's groups strongly supported protective laws and greater government expenditures for hospitals, schools, health education, recreational facilities, and factory inspectors. Nonetheless, the peculiar structure of Connecticut politics during the Progressive Era severely handicapped these efforts. Until the mid-1930s, control of the state government was held by a small group of pro-business, rural Republicans who vehemently opposed the advancement of women and their causes.[20]

Despite the high numbers of immigrants, Americans of British descent controlled the economy, according to Samual Koenig's analysis of Connecticut's economic life during the first three decades of the twentieth century. The only rivals to Yankee dominance were the Irish, but, as Koenig noted, "After all, it is large scale industry and finance which ultimately control the rest of our economic life, and these are primarily in the hands of British-Americans."[21]

The population shift did not bring about any fundamental changes in the political power structure either. Many of the immigrants could not or did not vote. Cities were underrepresented in the legislature because the state Constitution of 1818, though modified somewhat in the nineteenth century, provided that each town have two representatives in the House of Representatives. Thus, rural towns, controlled by pro-business, anti-labor Yankee Republicans, dominated state government. While rivalries were not uncommon within the GOP, party factions generally united in election years.[22]

The power of the GOP was enhanced by an increasingly weak and ineffectual Democratic party. The high tariff and sound money platform of the GOP in 1896 had attracted many conservatives away from the Democrats. Tensions between the growing number of urban Irish Democrats and the remaining old-line Yankees weakened the Democratic party's potential as a rural/urban coalition. Irish influence increased, but newer immigrants, courted by the Republicans, did not develop strong ties to the Democratic party until the 1930s.[23]

After the turn of the century, the Democratic party developed a somewhat more progressive image, though it did not endorse woman suffrage until 1916. Temporary splits in GOP ranks in 1910 and 1912 resulted in the election of Democratic Governor Simeon E. Baldwin. A former Yale professor and Chief Justice of the Connecticut Supreme Court, Baldwin was the only Democrat in the Statehouse between 1895 and 1931. During his two terms, the General Assembly passed a corrupt practices act, ratified the Seventeenth Amendment, established a state civil service system, and passed a workman's compensation act.[24]

With the Republicans reunited in 1914, their party regained the Statehouse. By then, the GOP was controlled by J. Henry Roraback, who headed the Republican State Central Committee from 1912 until 1937. At the peak of Boss Roraback's reign, wrote Connecticut historian Albert E. Van Dusen, "virtually every candidate and every patronage position in state politics had to be 'cleared' with 'J. Henry.' " As suffragists reported, even Democrats were recipients of Republican patronage, and thus were willing to follow the directives of the Republican machine. Cities, being corporations set up by the General Assembly, were subordinate to that governing body, and therefore even politicians in large cities hesitated to cross

Roraback on major issues. Finally, many of the state's influential newspapers, including the Hartford *Courant,* were staunchly Republican and unsympathetic to the efforts of reformers to democratize state government. The passage of special acts, which benefited corporations or localities, and the free-wheeling operation of the spoils system were seldom reported by the press. This made it difficult for the public to perceive the dangers of one-party government.[25]

The conservative Republicans conducted state affairs with frugality, eschewing deficit spending and a state income tax. Only sparingly did they allocate funds for hospitals, orphanages, state schools, factory inspectors, public works, and improvements in the cities. The machine opposed protective legislation, reapportionment, prohibition, and woman suffrage.[26]

Despite their conservative proclivities, many Connecticut citizens were critical of the machine-ridden government, and were concerned increasingly with the problems associated with rapid urban growth and industrialization. Among the strong advocates of social welfare legislation and the democratization of Connecticut politics during the Progressive Era were the suffragists, who believed that the state's political system was detrimental to the fulfillment of their aims to extend the political power of women: "Public opinion . . . is largely in favor of suffrage," said one woman. "Many of our representatives are opposed . . . because they fear it in politics," she added.[27]

The Women's Movement, 1909–1917

A great surge of feminist activity began in Connecticut around 1909 with the emergence in Greenwich and Hartford of a second generation of suffragists and strong suffrage organizations. The new leaders included Caroline Ruutz-Rees, Grace Gallatin Seton, and Valeria Hopkins Parker of Greenwich, and Emily Pierson and Katharine Houghton Hepburn of Hartford (see Appendix). Although they came to the suffrage struggle from a variety of backgrounds and experiences, these women adopted the rhetoric of their suffragist foremothers, proclaiming that simple justice demanded men not withhold from women their natural right to participate as equals in government, and indicating their concern for a wide range of issues, including child labor, prostitution, political corruption, and fair work standards. They believed that woman suffrage was a step in the direction of a more just and humane society.[28] Convinced that an effective campaign required statewide organizing and leadership, this new group "took possession" of the offices and machinery of the CWSA in 1910. Along with other women new to the suffrage cause, they built a movement which they dominated until suffrage was achieved, and then remained in the forefront of public life after 1920.[29]

Ruutz-Rees (b. 1865) was a graduate of Columbia University (MA and PhD, 1910). She was a distinguished scholar and headmistress of the prestigious Rosemary Hall School for Girls. Grace Gallatin Seton (b. 1872), a graduate of Packer Collegiate Institute and the wife of naturalist and writer Ernest Thompson Seton, was a well-known book designer, geographer, and traveler. One of the organizers of the Camp Fire Girls and a noted author, she had a particular interest in the condition of women in foreign lands. Valeria Hopkins Parker (b. 1879) was a physician "actively interested in anything pertaining to the welfare of women and children." She developed particular concerns for social hygiene, sex education, and woman suffrage and devoted her full time to these causes.[30]

The group in Hartford was led by Emily Pierson and Katharine Houghton Hepburn. Pierson (b. 1881) had just been graduated from Vassar (BA, 1907) and Columbia (MA, 1908) and begun teaching at Bristol (Connecticut) High School. She was interested in child welfare, education, social hygiene, and the problems of working women.[31]

Granddaughter of the founder of the Corning Glass Works, Hepburn (b. 1878) was graduated from Bryn Mawr (BA, 1899 and MA, 1900). After a brief teaching career in Baltimore, she and her husband, Dr. Thomas N. Hepburn, moved to Hartford in 1905. Both were concerned with social hygiene and the prevention and treatment of venereal disease. Soon after her arrival in Hartford, Hepburn, with neighbor Katherine Beach Day and her daughter Josephine Beach Bennett, organized local women to abolish the white slave trade and prostitution in the city. By means of marches and publicity, the women convinced the mayor to order an investigation which led to the houses being closed. An official report was issued, but Hepburn, backed by the CWSA, accused the press and certain politicians of suppressing it. They urged the "Mothers of Hartford" to hold their councilmen accountable for the matter.[32]

In October 1909, Emmeline Pankhurst visited Hartford for the first time. Attending this meeting were Hepburn and Pierson, who reportedly "received inspiration from Mrs. Pankhurst" and turned their energies toward building a suffrage campaign in their city. They organized the Hartford Political Equality League (later called the Hartford Equal Franchise League). The club "quickly attracted members and got into touch with the equally vigorous and enthusiastic young league in Greenwich." At the 1910 CWSA convention, Hepburn was elected president (1910-11 and 1913-17) and the other women became members of her board.[33]

This "younger, enthusiastic and militant group," wrote Annie Porritt, "infuse[d] new life" into the CWSA. Activities accelerated in the decade after 1910. By 1911, fourteen new suffrage leagues, including groups in New Haven and Bridgeport, were organized and affiliated with the CWSA, which claimed a membership of more than five thousand and an income of $3,966 for the year. By 1917, there were 32,000 members.[34]

Thousands of women participated in the drive for woman suffrage between 1910 and 1920. Of the vast majority, little or nothing is known. A few achieved fame as suffragists and were highly influential in the final years of the movement. Their suffrage experiences earned the respect of their colleagues, and their opinions were sought in top-level decision-making. The twenty-nine women cited in this study received wide publicity as leaders and activists in legislative work, public speaking, organizing, and fund-raising (see Appendix).[35]

All Connecticut suffrage leaders were middle- and upper-class women, and most of them had careers outside the home. Of the twenty-nine leaders, twelve were unmarried during the suffrage effort. This high percentage of single women suggests a conscious decision by some to avoid the frustrations of attempting to combine marriage, a family, and a career. Many had superior educations: a number had attended private schools; some had studied abroad; at least sixteen had attended college; there were three BAs, three MAs, two PhDs, and two MDs (another earned an MD in 1924); one had studied for the concert stage; four others had training beyond college. The group included writers, a poet and dramatist, physicians, artists, teachers, a geologist, a book designer and geographer, a social worker, and a professional lobbyist (see Appendix).

Several were paid organizers. The CWSA and the Connecticut Branch of the National Woman's Party [CNWP] had limited funds, however. Thus, women without independent means usually were prevented from full-time suffrage activity. This is one explanation for the preponderance of upper- and middle-class feminists in the suffrage leadership, and it does not mean that working women were not in sympathy with the movement. Connecticut factory workers actively supported woman suffrage.[36]

The personal lives and public activities of Connecticut's leaders attest to a wide range of interests and a commitment to change. Available evidence reveals that *all* viewed the vote as a tool for enacting social welfare legislation and reforming local, state, and national politics. Hardly naive, they expected to encounter relentless opposition to their programs. After 1920, they continued to be active in politics (see Appendix).

The escalation of suffrage activity in the state spurred the formation, in 1910, of the Connecticut Association Opposed to Suffrage, headed by Mrs. Daniel A. Markham of Hartford. Among the prominent women who opposed enfranchisement were Mrs. Samuel O. Prentice, wife of the Chief Justice of the Connecticut Supreme Court, Mrs. George McLean, wife of Connecticut's Republican senator, and Josephine Dodge, later a founder and president of the National Association Opposed to Woman Suffrage. Dodge was the daughter of Marshall and Esther Jewell, the Connecticut governor and his wife who had so enthusiastically welcomed the formation of the CWSA and endorsed the resolutions passed at its first convention in 1869. Esther Jewell was one of the signers of the call for that historic gathering.[37]

The antis appeared, along with the liquor interests, before legislative committees in 1917 and 1919. At the 1917 hearings, they opposed the granting of the vote to women in local option elections. The antis spoke *for* prohibition, but argued that woman suffrage was not the method by which the measure should be accomplished. At suffrage hearings in 1919, the antis accused the suffragists of radical sympathies and argued that suffrage would increase the feminist and Bolshevik vote in the state. After woman suffrage became the law of the land, a number of these antis became active in Republican politics in Connecticut.[38]

This study suggests that the Connecticut anti-suffrage women did not play a crucial role in obstructing the efforts of feminists in the early twentieth century. Rather, it was the Republican machine, allied with businessmen, farmers, and liquor interests—and backed by the anti-suffrage organization—that was largely responsible for the failure of suffrage bills and other progressive legislation in the General Assembly.[39]

After 1910, the expanding women's movement in Connecticut followed several paths. The suffragists put pressure on politicians and attempted to convince them that it was expedient to support women's causes. They sought the election of candidates favorable to women's rights and social welfare legislation. They worked virorously to enlarge membership in the suffrage association, and they publicized women's issues widely.

With automobile rallies, leafleting, letter-writing campaigns, petition drives, and speaking tours, they broadened their appeal to factory workers, immigrants, reformers, and politicians who opposed the Republican machine. Organizers reported visits with such groups as the state Sunday School Association, the Chamber of Commerce, the Grange, prominent party leaders, Jewish organizations, college professors, Black church women, corset workers, the Musicians Union, and many union locals. Suffrage measures were submitted at every session of the General Assembly, and suffragists testified at legislative hearings, demanding equal justice and arguing that women voters would support protective legislation, the abolition of political corruption, and temperance.[40]

These arguments were consistent with the tradition of reform which the Connecticut women's movement represented. Poor housing, urban squalor, unsafe and unsanitary working conditions, child labor, and other problems had become more widespread after the turn of the century. Suggesting its potential for political, economic, and social transformation, the women claimed that suffrage should become a high priority for concerned citizens.

The suffragists' link with prohibition cost the movement the loss of some potential supporters. Prohibition was always unpopular in the state and was opposed strongly by business, labor (including the Connecticut Federation of Labor), immigrants, the Republican bosses, and the liquor interests—brewery workers, saloon keepers, bartenders, and brewers. The CWSA officially backed prohibition, but, wisely, did not devote much attention to it in suffrage propaganda. Indeed, the suffragists were relieved when the prohibition question failed to achieve wide support, concluding that the wets no longer would fear women voting. The state did not ratify the Eighteenth Amendment.[41]

A matter which did divert public attention and energy away from suffrage was the entry of the United States into World War I in April 1917. Millions of women, including suffrage activists, volunteered for the war effort. The CWSA and local suffrage leagues sponsored many war activities, especially food conservation and fund-raising for overseas hospitals. Grace Seton went to France and organized a women's motor corps. Other suffrage leaders served as officials on state and national councils of defense (along with anti-suffragists).[42]

The feminists saw participation in war-related activities as an opportunity to demonstrate their willingness to share with men the burden of this monumental struggle. They clearly preferred to expend their energies exclusively on their own movement, but they did not want to invite accusations that working for suffrage at such a time was unpatriotic. The CWSA Central Committee on War Work issued resolutions to that effect shortly after the declaration of war: "Suffrage and patriotism are synonymous and . . . it is vitally important that our suffrage movement should not lose headway during the war." The committee, headed by Katharine Ludington, announced its strategy for war work: " . . . to hold together the suffrage voices of Connecticut by directing their war service [and] to 'get across' to the public mind the patriotic character of the suffrage movement and its attitude toward war."[43]

The Connecticut activists feared that excessive demands for industrial productivity would undermine laws passed by previous legislatures to protect women and child workers. This issue caused particular concern in the state, because with the outbreak of the European war in 1914, Connecticut had become one of the world's largest producers of arms and munitions. Thousands of women were employed in munitions factories, and since suffragists were "known to be in sympathy with all humanitarian legislation," the CWSA executive board assumed that the welfare of workers was an official responsibility of the organization. The war work committee was formed in part "to influence public opinion and legislatures" to maintain fair pay and work standards.[44]

From the feminists' perspective, the war increased the need for women in government decision-making. Thus, while war work was an important component of the 1917-1918 program of activities, the suffrage campaign intensified. Repeated failures to win the franchise through state action convinced the leaders that they should direct their efforts toward the federal amendment. The CWSA had strongly endorsed the "Six-Year Plan" unveiled by Carrie Chapman Catt at the 1916 convention of the National American Woman

Suffrage Association [NAWSA]. This new strategy called on NAWSA affiliates to work for state enfranchisement only in hopeful states. Other state associations should concentrate on working for the federal amendment by pressuring Senators and Congressmen to vote for the amendment and working for the election of state legislators favorable to ratification.[45]

The federal amendment was certainly not a new idea, but it had not been backed with vigorous political activity until 1913 when Alice Paul and Lucy Burns had taken over the Congressional Committee of the NAWSA. Paul's organization, the Congressional Union (CU), advocated that women should participate actively in partisan politics and that they should campaign—as the Woman's Party—against the Democrats in western suffrage states. The plan was to pressure Democratic President Woodrow Wilson and the Congress into endorsing the amendment. The NAWSA objected to this strategy and forced the withdrawal of the CU from its organization in 1914. The CU and the Woman's Party merged to form the National Woman's Party in 1916.[46]

From the beginning, Paul's approach had strong backing from Connecticut leaders. Hepburn and others had written to the NAWSA board in 1914 urging them to welcome the CU into the association. When a branch of the CU formed in Connecticut in 1915, two CWSA board members, Annie G. Porritt and Katherine Beach Day, joined the CU advisory board, while continuing their work with the CWSA. Another CWSA activist, Elsie Hill, served on the executive committee of the CU in 1914–1915.[47]

The CWSA board's uneasiness with NAWSA policy climaxed in the summer of 1917 after a number of NWP militants had been arrested and imprisoned for demonstrating outside the White House. The pickets and their sufferings created a great stir and made national headlines. These protests occurred at a time when the country's involvement in the war was upstaging the suffragists' efforts to extend democracy in their own country.[48]

Many Connecticut leaders agreed with these tactics, though the NAWSA did not, and the latter refused to condemn the harsh treatment of the pickets. Thus, in August and September of 1917, a number of the CWSA's prominent members, including President Hepburn, Treasurer Josephine Bennett, Press Secretary Annie Porritt, Membership Chairman Katherine Day, and four organizers, Emily Pierson, Elsie Hill, Katherine Mullen, and Catherine Flanagan, resigned their offices in the CWSA (but not their memberships) and joined the NWP. Bennett, Hill, and Flanagan were among the fourteen Connecticut pickets imprisoned between 1917 and 1919. The total number of demonstrators is not known, but 168 American women served jail sentences during the NWP campaign.[49]

Hepburn consented to stay in office until the CWSA convention in the fall "to prevent any possibility of the National Association sending some members . . . to speak . . . and try to discredit the Woman's Party." Although she believed that the work of the NAWSA had become "futile, academic, and out of date," she planned to keep "all controversial matters . . . in the background" so that the convention would "simply be a suffrage orgy." The presidency of the CWSA was offered to Vice-President Seton, who turned it down, and the office went to Katharine Ludington of Old Lyme. Another new member of the NWP, Valeria Parker, gave the keynote address at the CWSA convention.[50]

At the time of the resignations, the official statement of the CWSA board emphasized "a common aim both for those who are resigning and those who remain." The board noted that "the closest sympathy as to fundamental purpose still exists and . . . we welcome the fact that they will remain members of the association while not holding office." Hepburn remained on the CWSA executive board as president "ex officio." A member of the national executive committee of the NWP from 1917 until 1920 and chairman of the Connecticut Branch of the NWP in 1919 and 1920, Hepburn continued to maintain close ties with the CWSA and attended board meetings frequently until the amendment was ratified.[51]

Katherine Ludington, the new president of the CWSA, was a wealthy socialite from Old Lyme and a descendant of an old Connecticut family (see Appendix). A graduate of Miss Porter's School, she had traveled abroad, and become a portrait painter. Leader of the Old Lyme suffrage league and at the time of her election, chairman of the CWSA war committee, Ludington later told Ruth Dadourian that she had been "dragged kicking and screaming" into the CWSA presidency. She set up an apartment above the state headquarters in Hartford and traveled back and forth to Old Lyme in her limousine. Ludington worked tirelessly for the suffrage cause (and later for the League of Women Voters on the state and national levels, and the United Nations Association), and she did not hesitate to use her wealth and social connections to pressure state and national politicians to endorse woman suffrage. On taking office, she noted that she did not "subscribe" to the policy of the NWP, but she affirmed her support for the strategy which Hepburn and her board had been pursuing for the past year: "I believe the Federal Amendment to be the shortest route to Woman's Suffrage."[52]

While there is some evidence of friction between members of the CWSA and the NWP, it is likely that the differences had to do with personal style rather than ideology. Officially, relations remained cordial. Many of these women were personal friends, and they supported one another in their common effort. On one occasion the NWP sponsored a tea, and organizer Catherine Flanagan reported to Alice Paul that "all of the suffragists of the State Association in Hartford whom we had always been able to count upon for work came to the tea and pledged money and offered to help." In another instance, a CWSA organizer, under Ludington's instructions, sent canvas results to NWP worker Annie Porritt. When Porritt sent these on to NWP headquarters in Washington, she wrote:

> In using it do not make public in any way the fact that it was handed to us by the C.W.S.A. . . . There is a section on the Board that would make trouble for us all if they knew how amiable the President is to our Connecticut Branch. I promised not to get her into trouble concerning it.[53]

The overall goal of both groups was the same—to win support for the federal amendment. A number of NWP members worked outside Connecticut in more hopeful states. The CWSA, with its large membership and greater resources, did the bulk of the work within the state. The militancy of the NWP approach, while offensive to some women, invigorated the suffrage movement in Connecticut. "I felt that the Woman's Party was really the spearhead and then we could follow through," reported CWSA Executive Secretary Ruth McIntire Dadourian. "The more outrageous they were, the better off we were."[54]

Leaders of the state branch of the NWP, however, apparently made an effort to avoid identification with the "extremists" of the NWP so that the movement would remain united in the state. Moreover, the NWP policy of working against the Democratic party was inappropriate in Connecticut where political realities dictated that suffragists campaign against Republicans who, as Dadourian noted in her *History of the Year, 1919-1920,* "held independent views on the matter of suffrage from the national Republican leaders." At one time the two organizations considered setting up a joint committee to conduct ratification work; the committee was to be "entirely independent" of the NAWSA and NWP. They did not combine officially, however, and the CWSA did most of the work of the final drive for the vote.[55]

The relationship between the two suffrage groups in Connecticut is noteworthy, because most suffrage histories stress the conflicts and ideological distinctions between the NAWSA and NWP. The women who dominated the Connecticut struggle kept the movement united in their state. Conflicts between leaders of national suffrage organizations apparently did not filter down to state and local activists who shared common experiences and whose personal ties and commitments superceded their differences.[56]

That activists in both groups came together to celebrate the suffrage victory in 1920 and later worked together in the Connecticut League of Women Voters (CLWV), Birth Control League, Democratic party, and other groups gives further evidence of their fundamental commitment to the extension of women's political power and the advancement of humanitarian causes (see Appendix). The Connecticut suffrage organizations may be viewed less as branches of national associations than as relatively autonomous groups, consisting of women who readily accepted aid and advice from their national affiliates but who controlled the activities in their own state.[57]

Chapter II
Winning the Vote: The Final Years

A broad coalition comprised the suffrage movement in Connecticut during its final years. Women's clubs, church groups, labor unions, and professional organizations backed CWSA and NWP efforts to publicize issues, gather petitions, and lobby at the General Assembly. Suffragists came from all social and economic groups—rural Republicans, urban Blacks, society matrons, clerical workers, corset makers, prohibitionists, radical machinists, academics, unionists, industrialists, civic groups, and the unemployed. They were inspired and guided by the belief that greater political power for women was a fundamental right and would increase the potential for political, economic, and social reform.

The personal lives of prominent women reformers, both before and after suffrage, attest to their life-long commitment to a variety of causes, particularly to the extension of women's rights, the advancement of women in politics, and the improvement of the lives of working women and children. Connecticut feminists predicted that women voters would clean up politics, clear out the saloons, pass protective legislation, and inject a decidedly female element into politics. As the movement expanded, suffragists continued to claim that simple justice demanded the enfranchisement of one-half the population. Furthermore, they promised that enfranchisement would enable women to "get direct control in the outside world," and they reminded legislators that most "social laws . . . originated in women suffrage countries."[1]

The documents reveal that Connecticut suffragists understood that these arguments antagonized politicians. Nonetheless, they did not compromise their principles in order to win favor with conservative Republicans. They chose instead to demonstrate the increasing power of their movement in the hope that the "irreconcilables" would become convinced that failure to support woman suffrage would damage their party's and their own chances for re-election. This approach did have an impact. Many politicians ultimately endorsed ratification of the Nineteenth Amendment, only because they found it politically expedient to do so.

Women were far less successful in their attempts to unseat the rural political machine and to secure passage of social legislation. Indeed, the study of feminist efforts within the context of Connecticut political history provides ample evidence of the obstacles faced by women and by others seeking to democratize state politics and bring about a more equitable and humane system in the post-suffrage era.[2]

Recently collected life histories demonstrate the diversity of backgrounds and interests of Connecticut suffragists involved in the movement during its most active period, 1915-1920. Ruth McIntire Dadourian had participated in her first suffrage demonstration while a student at Radcliffe College. Later, a publicist for the National Child Labor Committee, she married a Trinity College professor and moved to Hartford. New to the area, with few acquaintances, she discovered the CWSA headquarters while on a shopping expedition. "I walked in, and, of course, they greeted me with open arms. Here was a young person who was interested and knew something about suffrage. Before I knew it, I was on the board," she explained.[3]

Edna Mary Purtell was an Irish Catholic whose parents worked in the cigar industry and were union activists and supporters of Eugene Debs. Purtell had become secretary of the tobacco strippers union at the age of sixteen and had been president of the Muriel McSweeney Club, a women's organization that supported Irish independence. While working as a file clerk at the Travelers Insurance Company, Purtell sometimes attended meetings of the Connecticut Branch of the NWP and helped to pass out leaflets in front of state headquarters in Hartford. "We wanted the eight-hour day and the forty-eight hour week," she explained in a 1980 interview. Though not a member of the NWP, she "appreciated the fact that the women who were being arrested were forcing people in this country to take notice." Thus, in August 1918, Purtell, then nineteen years old, took her vacation and journeyed to Washington to demonstrate with the NWP. Her train fare was paid by Katharine Hepburn who was unable to participate because she was pregnant with her sixth child. In Washington, she was arrested four times in one day, and she served five days on hunger strike in the Old District Jail, the youngest woman to do so during the two years of suffrage demonstrations.[4]

While she was in Washington, her fellow workers at the Travelers posted a "Votes for Women" sign in her office. When she returned, the president of the company warned her: "You know, Miss Purtell, you're liked very well here, but we don't want you to be talking about suffrage." Purtell reportedly assured him that she would "take care of [her] job." Nonetheless, she added, "Once I get in that elevator [or take a] coffee break . . . I'll talk about anything I want." He sent her back to her desk.[5]

Purtell's suffrage stand drew support from her family and her coworkers. Presumably few women were as bold and determined as young Edna Purtell, however; and not many could afford the time or money to spend on political activism. "You see, the working women had to look out for their jobs," Purtell later told Alice Paul. "There are a lot of women who would be here . . . but they can't afford it."[6]

The suffrage organizations were aware of this problem. At times, affluent individuals financed the activities of working women by paying their expenses and reimbursing them for their lost time. Primarily, workers demonstrated their support by passing suffrage resolutions to be submitted to Connecticut Congressmen and state legislators. For these endorsements, suffrage organizers worked vigorously in cities and factory towns, visiting work sites, standing on street corners, and meeting with state and local union leaders.[7]

At a 1918 meeting of the executive board of the CWSA, a suffragist reported that she had spoken in New Haven at a "war rally of colored women of the Congregational Church." The five hundred women voted to organize as "a colored suffrage league." Mrs. Richard Howell of the CWSA told of her "especially good work . . . in the colored district of Stratford." In May 1918, newly hired CWSA organizer Florence Ledyard Cross Kitchelt secured resolutions supporting suffrage from a number of Willimantic churches, including the official boards of the Methodist Church and the AME Zion Church, from the Prudential Board of the Baptist Church, and from a meeting of the Odd Fellows. She planned to pass out literature, "especially Catholic leaflets," at the mills.[8]

Kitchelt, a graduate of Wells College in 1897, had come to Connecticut after spending fifteen years in settlement work and three years as a suffrage organizer in Rochester, New York. She and her husband Richard Kitchelt, a lithographer, had no children; both

Socialists, they had independent careers. During the summer of 1918, Richard Kitchelt worked for the CWSA as a labor organizer. He reported reaching 2,689 men. Visiting 120 locals, he accumulated 111 suffrage resolutions. Three refused and the remainder were without quorum. Richard Kitchelt and four NWP representatives attended the annual convention of the Connecticut Federation of Labor in September 1918 where, after much debate, the delegates endorsed the federal amendment with only one dissenting vote.[9]

The friendly and mutually supportive relations between the NWP and the International Association of Machinists is further evidence of the suffragists' ties with workers, during the war years and in the early post-war period. That the NWP had decided to appeal to the Bridgeport workers at that time is significant. One of the world's major arsenals in World War I, the city was experiencing serious labor trouble during August and September of 1918. A dispute over standardization of job classification and wages of machinists and toolmakers had resulted in a walk-out of thousands of munitions workers. Represented by the International Association of Machinists (IAM), the men and women were protesting the discrepancy between the accepted union scale (which the federal government was paying employees at the Navy yard in Bridgeport) and their own lower wages. The United States Labor Board presented an offer which IAM Local Agent Sam Lavit and his union refused to accept. Backed by IAM national president, William Johnston, President Woodrow Wilson ordered the workers to return. He threatened to bar strikers from other employment and rescind their draft exemptions. This ended the strike.[11]

The munitions strikes of the summer of 1918 made national headlines. Bridgeport, described by the *New York Times* as "the greatest little war purveyor in America," had experienced serious social and economic problems, including spectacular population growth, inflation, and shortages of housing, factory space, schools, and recreational facilities. Pressure to produce had prompted factory owners to lengthen hours and demand increased productivity from their workers, whose jobs often involved hazardous work with explosives and poisonous chemicals. Although workers' problems were severe, strikes were considered radical and unpatriotic.[12]

The NWP had a particular attraction to the IAM, since the NWP was campaigning against the Machinists' bitter opponent, Woodrow Wilson. Clara Louise Rowe and Elsie Mary Hill were in Bridgeport during the strike, and on September 7, 1918 they addressed a street corner rally of workers. Hill recounted her experiences as a White House picket and exhorted her audience to pressure Connecticut's Senators to "come across." Rowe asserted that the extension of suffrage was "a war measure"—proof that America, unlike Germany, was a democracy. The *Bridgeport Herald* reported a "generous response" to the women's request for money, "chiefly from men." The newspaper announced Hill's plans to speak at another mass meeting of men war workers on the following Monday and quoted her parting comment: "The State and the town . . . are not very friendly . . . . But organized labor is always our friend."[10] At another meeting, Hill reported speaking to five thousand members of the IAM.

On September 13, 1918 Hill met with the IAM auxiliary and discussed the National Woman's Party "watchfire" demonstrations in Washington. Of those attending, twenty volunteered to support the NWP protest in the nation's capitol. (Two of the twenty were IAM members and the others belonged to the auxiliary.) Noteworthy is the participation of Mrs. Sam Lavit, wife of the Bridgeport IAM Local Agent, who also volunteered. In the words of a Corset Workers Union member, she was going to Washington "because I want to be considered a person. As it is now I am not a person. I am not anything."[13]

When the strikes ended, the cordial relationship between the Machinists and the NWP continued. On January 5, 1919 NWP's Josephine Beach Bennett, speaking at a meeting in Bridgeport, convinced a number of the women workers in attendance to join the NWP-sponsored protest on Connecticut Day, when Connecticut logs would be used to burn copies of President Wilson's speeches. The protesters wanted to remind Wilson, who was in the midst of peace negotiations with the European powers, that although a war had been fought for democracy abroad, American women lacked political equality. The factory workers stayed at the NWP's Washington headquarters. "They don't know whether we are working women or millionaires, and treat us all alike," reported Mrs. Weaver and Elsie Vervane, president of the Bridgeport Ladies Machinist Union. Vervane had also participated in the NWP demonstrations in the fall of 1918, and this time was arrested with Josephine Bennett and four other Bridgeport munitions workers. The women spent several days in jail, and went on a hunger strike that lasted ninety-four hours.[14]

While the women were serving their sentences, Sam Lavit told Katherine Day that "there are more women who would like to go [to Washington], but we have not the money with which to send them." Upon her release from prison, Bennett reported to Alice Paul:

> [Lavit has] done more for the National Woman's Party in Connecticut than any other man. He is well known by government officials in Washington and the union he represents (the Machinists) they stand more in awe of than of any other in the nation. And the Bridgeport local is the most respected and feared of any. It was most excellent having Mrs. Vervane and the others call at the Executive Offices on account of the huge organization back of them.[15]

After the November 1918 armistice, Bridgeport's war boom came to a sudden halt, and the city suffered from severe unemployment. At a mass meeting of Bridgeport's unemployed, who were demanding five dollars per week in unemployment compensation, Josephine Bennett and NWP activists Louise Bryant and Clara Wohl were featured speakers. Bryant told of her recent trip to the Soviet Union. Wohl and Bennett spoke in favor of a woman suffrage resolution. The meeting unanimously passed a resolution, sent to President Wilson, demanding "immediate action by you on woman suffrage," and resolving that the "working men and women of Bridgeport, members of District 55, IAM, in mass meeting assembled do stand united" behind the five women members of the Machinists' Union who served sentences in the Washington jail. At the same meeting, Sam Lavit was charged by police with selling a banned pamphlet, "Won a War—Lost a Job." Another Bridgeport man, Samuel Krawchuk, a Russian, was arrested for distributing a leaflet, "Free Our Political Prisoners," issued by the "League for Amnesty of Political Prisoners of New York."[16]

The Bridgeport activities added a number of supporters to the suffrage movement, but connections with labor unions clearly offended the politicians in power. Nonetheless, there is no evidence that Connecticut suffragists used anti-labor propaganda to advance their own cause. The issue of courting the unions, while attempting to win over Connecticut Senator George McLean, was considered at a CWSA board meeting. The Minutes noted that Mary Bulkley urged the board to seek more resolutions from labor unions. Mrs. Russell then "opposed this on the ground that it would antagonize rather than influence Mr. McLean in the right way." A discussion followed and, significantly, Bulkley's views prevailed.[17]

The Connecticut women refused to resort to nativist arguments in order to curry favor with middle class voters, although such an approach was suggested to the state association in a NAWSA memorandum dated May, 1918. A list of "POINTS TO BE STRESSED IN MASS MEETINGS AND IN PUBLICITY" included the following:

> Point 6. A hundred percent American Republic will not deny its women the political liberty that monarchs have extended . . . .
> Point 9. We are to send million[s] of young men out of the country, leaving their families without a voter, while men too disloyal to be trusted with war work are trusted to vote. The enfranchisement of women by the federal amendment means to give the country a patriotic vote of defense.[18]

Indeed, the CWSA's own list of "ARGUMENTS" in 1919 mentioned only the rights of women in a political democracy and the fact that the national parties had endorsed woman suffrage.[19]

On only one occasion did a blatantly nativist argument appear in the Connecticut documents: "We believe that in this crazy condition of the world today, that if the world is to be stabilized it must be done by the best agencies we have; those of our population who have been properly educated and Americanized."[20] Significantly, the speaker was a man, Isaac Ullman, a long-time supporter of suffrage, a leading Republican, the boss of New Haven, and a representative of the Men's Ratification Committee (MRC), a Republican organization which aimed to convince the machine and Governor Marcus Holcomb to recognize the inevitability of woman suffrage. Holcomb was refusing to call a special emergency legislative session to vote on the ratification of the federal amendment. The MRC believed the amendment would become law with or without the help of Connecticut, and they feared that enfranchised women would hold the GOP responsible if the amendment was not ratified in time for the 1920 fall elections. These arguments ultimately persuaded the intractable Connecticut Senators to endorse the calling of the special session. It would be inappropriate to attribute this new approach to the women who led the suffrage effort.[21]

The avoidance of nativist arguments by Connecticut suffragists is significant. While historians have found examples of nativism in other documents, it cannot be assumed that most feminists subscribed to them. Such arguments might well have appealed to Yankee politicians who held the fate of the suffrage question in their hands. Nevertheless, Connecticut suffragists apparently rejected this approach, suggesting a reluctance to compromise their democratic principles.[22]

Enfranchisement became the focus of the Connecticut women's movement, and the women continued to make clear also that suffrage was needed in order to topple the machine. "Measures passed at [the machine's] behest are frequently for private profit rather than for public good," the CWSA announced. Thus, they concluded, "we can never hope to carry out our programme as long as we have to appeal to a legislature controlled by the Republican machine."[23]

Although they decided to endorse only the presidential suffrage bill before the 1919 General Assembly, the CWSA urged all suffragists to attend hearings on other measures, including the minimum wage, regulating day nurseries, and factory inspection. They appointed a special committee "to study and examine" social bills before the 1919 legislature and to issue a weekly bulletin informing suffragists of the progress of each bill.[24]

The women were dissatisfied with the 1919 session in part because it failed to pass the suffrage bill. At the close of the session, the CWSA issued another statement entitled "The Republican Machine," which blamed the machine for failing to pass ten bills "strongly supported by the women of Connecticut, for the protection of women and children." The statement specifically mentioned legislation which would have shortened the work week of women and children to fifty hours, provided forty-five minute lunch periods, forbidden children under sixteen to work during school hours, and set up a minimum wage commission. The author of this lengthy analysis of the hand of the machine in the 1919 session was particularly angered by the politicians' padding of appropriations with patronage:

> The machine saw in the [Widow's Pension Bill] an opportunity for a job for one of its faithful members and a substitute bill

was drawn up in committee providing for a commissioner at $3,000 a year and expenses, with assistants to be named by him. It seems to have been of less importance to relieve the widows than to provide patronage for the machine, for in this substituted bill, the relief to be granted is wholly inadequate . . . . The cost of administering the Widow's Pension Law is out of all proportion to the amount of money that goes to the widows and their children.[25]

The women were dismayed, moreover, at the "volume of special laws," granting excessive powers to private interests, especially to the Connecticut Light and Power Company, "of which Mr. J. Henry Roraback is one of the original incorporators." Particularly alarming to them was the alteration of the general married women's property law of the state. The new law "deprived [married women] of the control of their real estate—if this real estate is needed by the Connecticut Light and Power Company." The control was given "absolutely to their husbands."[26]

Such a wide range of legislative and political concerns characterized the final period of suffrage agitation and made clear that, once enfranchised, these women intended to pursue their causes with continued vigor. The adoption of a citizen education program during this period also reflected this commitment. For the last three years of the movement, CWSA activist Nancy Schoonmaker devoted herself to citizenship education, in order to develop "a stronger civic sense in women . . . and . . . a more active share in political parties as the method by which political reformers [sic] are accomplished." Schoonmaker organized citizenship courses, visited scores of communities to speak with civic leaders and urged local women to help with voter registration drives. She encouraged women to join political parties, though citizenship activity itself was deliberately non-partisan. The CWSA Citizenship Committee was a forerunner of the Connecticut League of Women Voters (CLWV).[27]

Meanwhile the prospects for passage of the federal amendment grew brighter. The CWSA sought endorsement by Congressmen and Senators and the election of a state legislature in favor of ratification. Organized in every district, the women actively pursued pro-suffrage endorsements from parties and individuals. They readily publicized indications of support for suffrage by political candidates. In describing tactics for the 1918 election, CWSA President Ludington told the board, "The association . . . will make its appeal equally to both parties." Suffragists who joined the parties were encouraged to campaign for suffrage from within. Most Democrats endorsed suffrage in 1918, but Republican leaders, as usual, remained opposed, a fact that was given "wide publicity."[28]

However, the machine men still turned deaf ears to arguments based on simple justice, and were probably worried by the women's promises of political uplift after they got the vote. Moreover, to demonstrate to the machine and to Republicans at large that support for suffrage was politically expedient was difficult; Connecticut Republicans had little competition for power.

Two distinctive political tactics emerged in this election campaign. The CWSA offered tangible support to pro-suffrage candidates, suggesting that they could act as a non-partisan political force to influence the outcome of elections. Furthermore, some women had begun to work for their political goals *within* the established parties.

The suffrage organizations continued to encourage their members to pressure their Senators and Congressmen to vote for the amendment. Both Connecticut Senators were strongly anti and were unreceptive to the deputations of women who pleaded their cause. To persuade Brandegee and McLean, women argued that a pro-suffrage sentiment would be beneficial to the Republican party. When the United States House of Representatives finally passed the amendment in January 1919, four of Connecticut's five Congressmen voted with the majority; the only Democrat, Augustin Lonergan, was opposed. Brandegee and McLean voted nay when the amendment passed the Senate in June 1919.[29]

The suffragists' 1918 campaign also resulted in the election of a new General Assembly with a decidedly favorable sentiment toward the federal amendment, if not toward state legislation. Unfortunately the 1919 legislative session adjourned before lawmakers considered ratification of the Nineteenth Amendment. (The United States Senate did not pass the bill until after the Connecticut session had adjourned.) Because the legislature would not meet again until January 1921, the governor would have to order a special session to consider ratification. Holcomb, who had been *commended* for supporting woman suffrage in 1902, adamantly refused to sound the call, claiming that such an action was permissible only in an emergency. Some Connecticut suffragists, notably Hepburn and Bennett, were skeptical of the prospects for changing Holcomb's mind, but the leaders of the NAWSA and the NWP exhorted the state affiliates to do everything possible to bring Connecticut into line. Thus, women from both organizations participated in the fifteen-month ratification drive.[30] Throughout the summer and fall of 1919, the suffragists attempted to convince Holcomb to call the special session. They presented him with the signatures of 103,000 Connecticut women and hired a publicity bureau with three paid professionals from New York. Holcomb was besieged by petitions from the Republican and Democratic parties and from each house of the legislature, but still held back. Moreover, the powerful Republican State Central Committee refused to pressure him to call the session.[31]

At the CWSA Jubilee Convention, held in Bridgeport in November 1919, to celebrate the sixtieth anniversary of the organization, the delegates adopted a resolution which pointed to a "small group of Connecticut Republicans," who were "hindering the calling of a special session of the legislature." The association resolved "to concentrate its opposition against this small group within the Republican party." Denying any departure from its "traditional policy of non-partisanship," the CWSA declared that while it was "not backing either political party, nor [was] it affiliating with any group within a party," the CWSA was "encouraging" women to give "thought to what their political affiliations are to be." Though "not opposed to having members join the women's organizations of the political parties," the delegates urged "that until Connecticut women are enfranchised, loyalty to suffrage shall take precedence of loyalty to a state party."[32]

The CWSA board suggested that Republican suffragists take the following approach: "that they work for the National Republican Party and join the Republican women's organizations for that purpose." However, they should "not work for the Connecticut Republican Party until it changes its attitude toward ratification of the Federal Suffrage Amendment." They pointedly noted that "the state Democratic party . . . has a suffrage plank in its platform and favors ratification." Thus, as the suffragists approached the day when they would be able to elect public officials, they were confronting their enemies on a single issue—their position on woman suffrage. They were determined to convince the men that they had more to gain by supporting ratification than by obstructing the calling of the special session.[33]

On Ludington's urging, pro-suffrage Republicans organized the Republican Men's Ratification Committee, which presented the governor with arguments for calling the special session. These politicians, wanting to take *credit* for ratification, expected to be rewarded for their loyalty to the suffrage cause: "While I don't want to compare the women with the colored man . . . , the fact is that colored vote is still largely Republican, not because of what the Republicans are doing for him, but because the Republicans are responsible for his vote." The message was clear: Support votes for women so that the Republicans could retain their control and probably manipulate the new female voters.[34]

The emphasis during this phase of the drive was on the mobilization of public opinion. The women sought to create such a clamor that the men in power would have to yield to popular demand for the special session. With the help of prominent national and state Republican leaders, the Connecticut suffragists "intended to get the vote through the men of their own state." Though they believed that ratification was inevitable in any case, they were determined to put Connecticut on the list of ratifying states.[35]

This campaign had an impact. In March, Brandegee told NWP worker Helena Hill Weed that Connecticut should ratify because suffrage was inevitable. He feared that continued opposition could arouse the antagonism of the new voters. By that time, McLean also had endorsed the session. The Republican state convention adopted a resolution requesting the session. (Both Democratic and Republican convention platforms also included a number of planks on social welfare legislation.) Yet, although the politicians were recognizing the expediency of endorsement, the women were angry. The state Republican convention had "returned to power the very men who had most bitterly opposed us and who were at that time standing in the way of a special session."[36]

On March 22, 1920, Washington became the thirty-fifth state to ratify, and the national suffrage organizations included Connecticut on their lists of "hopefuls" for the thirty-sixth (and final) ratification. Holcomb announced "that persistent appeals do not constitute an emergency," but on April 10 he invited the presentation of proofs of an emergency situation. The CWSA designated May 3 as the beginning of "emergency week." They brought in women from the forty-eight states—a "Suffrage Emergency Corps"—to make speaking tours throughout the state. A mass meeting was held at the capitol. The Men's Ratification Committee presented Holcomb with a formal request for the special session. Holcomb was unmoved.[37]

The events of 1919-1920 demonstrate that the mobilization of large numbers of women *and* men for political purposes would not necessarily affect government policy. Suffragists were rendered powerless because the Connecticut political system made it possible for a few to govern without regard for public interest or public opinion. The ratification drive suggests that even if "the mass of female citizens" acted "in a cohesive and committed manner" (as historian William H. Chafe charged they failed to do after enfranchisement), a system which severely limited popular access to political decision-making could thwart even the most determined attempts to bring about change.[38]

Because of the relentless opposition of Holcomb and his machine backers, the CWSA board decided to employ more drastic measures. On June 3, 1920, they voted "to oppose the Republican Party in the State in the coming campaign, with the exception of those men who were the tried and true friends of suffrage and of those who would come out and work for a special session." Thus, the CWSA abandoned its official non-partisan position, "in the main to prove to the machine that it would be a far wiser thing to do to get the suffrage issue out of the way before the . . . election."[39]

Moreover, a number of the state's leading Republican women issued their own statement: "We will not help the Republican Party . . . by contributing money, or speaking in the campaign until the 36th state has ratified and our position as voters is made secure." With this "no vote, no money" pledge, partisan women were fulfilling the hopes of reform-minded suffragists that women would not allow party loyalty to take precedence over their social welfare and feminist goals. The decision to withhold financial support from anti-suffragists exemplified the dilemma which Connecticut women faced throughout the movement. They were announcing that women would not sacrifice their principles in order to gain favor with men in power. Consequently, they provoked the politicians to resist women's political struggles even more vehemently.[40]

During the summer of 1920, the most intensive struggle on the national scene centered in Tennessee. Despite strong opposition, Tennessee ratified, and the Nineteenth Amendment became the law on August 26, 1920.[41]

After the amendment had been ratified by the required thirty-six states, Holcomb called an emergency session for September 14, 1920, with the expressed purpose of setting up the machinery for registering the new voters. He warned the legislature to "restrict itself to the business outlined in the call." In the midst of plans for the session, some antis charged that the Tennessee legislature had acted illegally. Ratification by Connecticut would remove all doubt as to the legality of the amendment. Fearing that the ensuing court battle could bring into question the validity of the results of the upcoming elections, Connecticut politicians urged the General Assembly to ratify.[42]

When the September 14 session convened, Holcomb called for an adjournment, so he could issue another call for the purpose of ratification. The assembly ignored his request, voted to ratify immediately, pursued other business, then adjourned. The lawmakers met again on September 21 and ratified the amendment twice more.[43]

Thus, the fifty-one-year effort was over. Yet, the women saw their victory not as the end of their struggle, but as a step toward a more democratic and humane society:

> Now what had it all been for? Do you think that Miss Ludington and that those who led the work before her could have carried it on with such indomitable spirit only in order that women might go to the polls once a year and drop their ballot in a box? Do you think they could have done it if they had not believed that women would use their votes to wipe out the injustices in the world—the injustices between man and man and between woman and man—to lift intolerable burdens from motherhood and childhood?[44]

The documents reveal that Connecticut suffragists understood that enfranchisement alone was not sufficient to transform politics and society. Yet, wrote Ruth Dadourian, they believed that the struggle for women's voting rights had "always been educational both to ourselves and our opponents, who have learned that women are a force to be counted with." In the opinion of Connecticut feminists, who were already meeting to plan the future, the women's movement was far from over. "Even if we wanted to could we possibly escape the responsibility of victory?" asked Dadourian. Only one question remained. How could the women exert their influence most effectively?[45]

Chapter III
The Responsibility of Victory

*The world, half yours, demands your care,
Waken and come!
Make it a woman's world: safe, fair,
Garden and home.*

Charlotte Perkins Gilman[1]

In the post-suffrage era, Connecticut women continued their efforts to extend their political power and weaken the power of the conservative Republicans. Working particularly through the League of Women Voters, they advocated measures to raise the legal status of women and to improve living and working conditions of their fellow citizens. Their political education programs equipped women with information about governmental structure and procedures and about tactics for applying political pressure for social legislation.

In the fall of 1920, the CWSA engaged in three major activities. It continued its citizenship education program; launched a voter registration drive; and, almost unanimously, voted to direct the full force of the organization toward the defeat of Senator Frank Brandegee. Members decided not to disband the CWSA and to postpone formation of the non-partisan Connecticut League of Women Voters until after the November elections.

Immediately the CWSA began to work for legislation to expedite registration—the transfer of school voters to the regular lists and the extension of the registration period to accommodate the large numbers of new applicants. The activists encouraged new voters to enroll in political parties. In some areas, the parties themselves were helping with voter registration, and the CWSA willingly relinquished this effort.

The desire to expand the voters' lists and swell party ranks was an inevitable outcome of the suffrage struggle. Nonetheless, allowing party regulars to carry on the work of voter registration weakened the potential for female solidarity. The Republican party was predictably more active in this endeavor than the Democrats, and

37

there is no evidence that third parties made any effort to enroll women.[2]

A crucial matter in the late summer and early fall of 1920 was the admission of women to town caucuses where party decision-making occurred and where the selection of candidates for local office and for convention delegates was made. Here women met resistance. One woman reported to the CWSA board that "the machine had given no opportunity to the women to vote" at Republican caucuses. She was convinced that the party leaders "were afraid that the men would let the women vote and so upset the cut and dried program."[3]

The women debated the question of joining the parties and taking positions within the parties. CWSA President Ludington suggested that "women at present sit tight and do more thinking before taking positions within the party." They debated whether women should "get into the party and work for reform inside" or "hold a position as independent voters and reform from outside." The board noted that women "were to have no voice in electing the delegates to the Republican or Democratic conventions." Moreover, they would have "no voice directly on choice of candidates [or] on the drawing of platforms." Under such circumstances, Ludington could only urge the activists to attend party conventions as observers and express their opinions on issues and candidates wherever possible.[4]

Ludington and the board were fully aware of the barriers which male politicians would place in their paths. Women needed "a status [to] make our contribution to the world," she claimed. According to Ludington, this had been the "purpose of the suffrage agitation but this purpose was not fully completed. The world was not yet fif[ty]-fifty in regard to men's views and women's views." Nor was "women's voice yet fifty-fifty within the political parties."[5]

Therefore, how were women "to get most weight for the women's point of view?" Ludington asked. She encouraged the formation of a "non-partisan organization to re-enforce the women and their work within all parties and to keep the women together." This was to be the purpose of the League of Women Voters—an organization to serve as "a clearing house for women's work and a meeting ground for the women." Through such non-partisan pressure groups, Ludington hoped to sustain the unity of women on issues which concerned them.[6]

The feasibility of this strategy was tested in the anti-Brandegee campaign. The decision to work for Brandegee's defeat received wide and often negative publicity. One formerly pro-suffrage paper called the campaigners "a noisy and active clique of . . . professional suffragists . . . who are shoving sex so conspicuously into politics" and were "actuated by little else than the spirit of huff." The CWSA was joined in this effort by a group from Yale University who opposed Brandegee on grounds of his hostility to the League of Nations and to all social legislation.[7]

In their publicity the women attacked the Senator's consistently pro-business votes, his emphasis on military preparedness, and his machine connections, concluding that it was "impossible for a man of his temperament and record ever to represent women or to give any aid to the measures that women desire to see passed." The state Republican organization worked hard for Brandegee, not only defending his record but also claiming that a split ticket would invalidate ballots. The campaign took an interesting twist when antisuffragists branded Brandegee a traitor because he had belatedly supported ratification of the Nineteenth Amendment—after becoming convinced (with the help of suffragist propaganda) that such support was politically expedient. Some women reportedly were moved to support him "on account of much persecution," though most suffragists stood "pat on his record" and did not "hesitate to denounce him." For many voters, including suffragist Corinne Alsop, already active in the Republican party, the past was not an issue, and their traditional Republican loyalties overrode their distaste for the Senator.[8]

In the 1920 Republican landslide, Brandegee was returned to the Senate. The odds for crushing him had been slim. Along with pro-business conservatives and advocates of limited government, Brandegee had cultivated the support of many ethnic voters, especially the Irish, Germans, and Italians, who were hostile to the peace settlement. Moreover, Brandegee's Democratic opponent, Congressman Augustin Lonergan, had a record similar to the Senator's: he had voted against woman suffrage in the House of Representatives, and he had given only lukewarm support to the Versailles Treaty. The entrenched power of the GOP in the state, the weak state Democratic organization, and the anti-Democratic national mood undermined the CWSA effort. The sentiment expressed by a Stratford woman in explaining her refusal to vote for Lonergan probably typified that of many citizens: "Not that I love the Republicans more but that I love the Democrats less."[9]

In the opinion of CWSA leaders, however, the anti-Brandegee campaign had accomplished two goals. Their publicity had forced debate of issues of importance to women and had put Brandegee on the defensive. (He had protested that he was "not reactionary, not unprogressive, and not opposed . . . to woman suffrage except that he did not think the women of the state wanted it.") Explained campaign leader Ruth McIntire Dadourian in a 1980 interview: "We wanted to run him back.... We knew we couldn't defeat him.... He'd always led the ticket." Brandegee ran more than 25,000 votes behind his ticket in the election. After the election, the suffragists remained optimistic that politicians would consider seriously women's votes in the future. Yet the Brandegee victory made clear the enormous difficulty which organized women could expect to face in their efforts to affect the outcome of elections in Connecticut.[10]

After suffrage, women's organizations renewed their attack on political corruption, criticized conservative Republican rule, and demanded a larger role in party decision-making. The suffrage leaders did not challenge the centrality of the party system, but they "had much experience with party machines," observed one CWSA member, and they "knew the evils in Connecticut."[11] Many joined the Democratic, Progressive, Farmer-Labor, and Socialist parties, which they felt were more compatible with their political views. Others remained Independent (see Appendix).

The parties, of course, welcomed female registrants in the hope of "taking over" the women's vote, but the GOP in particular kept reform-minded, independent women from obtaining key positions. Former CWSA officer and president of the CLWV Mary Bulkley later observed, "In some cases [women] have been made tools of party bosses." Indeed, the Republicans appointed former leaders of the anti-suffrage movement to the state central committee with the responsibility for overseeing its voter education program. Corinne Alsop, the founder of the League of Republican Women, objected, but to no avail.[12]

Events in the early post-suffrage era gave women every reason to be skeptical of their chances for exerting influence from within the parties as then constituted, so it is not surprising that a major thrust of the work of the CLWV was government reform and citizenship education. The League emphasized that principle should take precedence over party affiliation. Countless League activists campaigned for non-partisanship in local politics and were instrumental in revising town charters in the decades following enfranchisement.[13]

A fundamental belief of the women's movement in Connecticut

since its founding in 1869 was that government should take a larger role in safeguarding the lives of its citizens. Thus, during the period encompassed in this study, women supported bills providing shorter hours of work in industry, widows' pensions, regulation of child labor, the closing of houses of prostitution, funds for schools and hospitals, prohibition, and other reforms. After 1920, Connecticut women continued these efforts and added numerous other matters to their list, including juvenile courts, maternity and child health care, the liberalization of birth control laws, improved roads, and the control of pollution. Women were especially interested in the welfare of children and supported improved day care facilities, organized Girl Scout troops, set up recreation centers, and crusaded against child labor.[14]

Women of varying backgrounds and party affiliations often worked together for these ends. In New Haven, for example, Republican Edith Valet Cook, Democrat Laura Belle Reed McCoy, and Socialist Celia Duhan Rostow met while working for the Girl Scouts. These three served together on numerous boards and commissions in their efforts to help the children of their city. Cook, a Yale Law School graduate and Republican legislator (1927–29 and 1957–59), directed the Connecticut Child Welfare Association for more than fifty years. McCoy, a native American who lived in the Black community, was a practical nurse and founded the first Girl Scout troop for Black children in the United States. She later became the first non-white woman to serve on the New Haven Board of Alderman (1941–43). Rostow, in contrast, was the Socialist Party candidate for Connecticut Secretary of the State in 1934, in addition to her volunteer work with the Girl Scouts and the Jewish Community Center. (During the late 1960s, she served as a VISTA Volunteer in South Boston.) Cook, McCoy, and Rostow remained friends and associates for more than a half century.[15]

International relations was another special interest of Connecticut women. During World War I, they had argued that increasing the participation of women in government would advance the cause of peace. After the war, they endorsed arms reduction and campaigned actively for the League of Nations, the World Court, and other institutions which promoted international cooperation. Among the leaders of the peace movement were former suffrage leaders Florence Kitchelt and Josepha Whitney. Through membership in the League of Women Voters, many others were drawn to the peace movement.[16]

Continuity marks the history of the ideas and goals of the women's movement in Connecticut. Suffragists were convinced that enfranchisement would constitute an important step forward in securing social legislation, democratizing politics, and promoting world peace. Life-long commitment to these goals characterized the women who were part of the women's movement in the state. They understood that the accomplishment of their objectives would occur only with persistent organizational efforts. As they had belonged before 1920 to a variety of reform-oriented groups, so they worked in similar organizations after suffrage. Most joined the CLWV; many became active in political parties, particularly in women's organizations within the parties; others ran for office; some held elective and appointive office; and those elected to the legislature formed their own organization, the Order of Women Legislators (OWLs) which became a support group and educational forum for office-holders. Many women combined these activities (see Appendix).[17]

Josephine Hamilton Maxim was one such woman. Officer of the CWSA, founder of the CLWV, she ran unsuccessfully for the state senate in 1920 on the Democratic ticket, and in the same year was an alternate delegate to the Democratic national convention. She later became an important leader in Hartford politics, holding numerous positions on local health and welfare commissions and the school board. In a 1980 interview, her daughter Percy Maxim Lee (who served four terms as president of the National League of Women Voters, 1950-58) reflected on her mother's life-long career in politics:

> I think she, like a great many women of that era, determined that if you wanted to get anything done that would be of a reform sort—in any field—you had to get into politics to get it done . . . . She spent an awful lot of time trying to get done the sorts of things that she thought would be beneficial to the people of Hartford . . . . She was very much persuaded that women must assume this responsibility.[18]

A survey of the lives of former Connecticut suffrage leaders about whom data is available has revealed that all remained active in public affairs after 1920 (see Appendix). Katharine Ludington held various offices on the state and national levels in the LWV and worked vigorously for public support for the United Nations in the

1940s. She also remained an influential figure in the political life of her home town of Old Lyme.[19]

Caroline Ruutz-Rees was a trustee of the League of Nations Association and active in the CLWV and the Democratic party. She served on the Democratic National Committee and was woman chairman for Connecticut under the National Recovery Administration of the New Deal. In the 1930s, Ruutz-Rees allowed the Greenwich Committee for Maternal Health to use a house owned by the Rosemary Hall School—when she was still headmistress—as headquarters for an illegal birth control clinic.[20]

Writer and traveler Grace Gallatin Seton studied and wrote about women in foreign cultures and presided over the National League of American Pen Women (1926-28 and 1930-32). As chairman of letters of the National Council of Women (1933-38), she spearheaded the establishment of the Biblioteca Femina, a library of women's writings from all over the world. An active Republican, she worked for the equal status of women on the Republican National Committee.[21]

Emily Pierson, who received her MD degree from Yale Medical School in 1924 at the age of forty-three, served as director of health and school physician in her home town of Cromwell for more than thirty years. Pierson, known as a specialist on life in socialist countries, spoke frequently about her trips to the Soviet Union and the People's Republic of China where she visited her long-time friend, Anna Louise Strong, the radical journalist. Pierson was one of those who helped to reorganize the Connecticut Branch of the National Woman's Party in 1922.[22]

Annie Porritt, an officer of the CLWV until her death in 1932, was active in the Farmer-Labor party in the early 1920s and, with Dr. Valeria Parker and Dr. Thomas Hepburn, in the field of public health and social hygiene. She joined the birth control movement after suffrage was won. Asserting that "all working women have a right to information, a right to control the size of their families," Porritt, along with Katherine Day and Josephine Bennett, set up the state's first organization for the liberalization of birth control laws.[23]

Katharine Houghton Hepburn became the "leading light" of the birth control movement in Hartford. Connecticut's laws against dissemination of birth control information and the use and sale of birth control devices were particularly stringent. In the 1930s, Hepburn organized the Hartford Maternal Health Center, one of several illegal birth control clinics which operated in open defiance of the law until a police raid in Waterbury in 1939. A close associate of Margaret Sanger, Hepburn appeared frequently as an advocate of birth control before Congressional committees and the Connecticut legislature. Until her death in 1951, she remained one of the leading birth control activists in the United States. (Despite years of lobbying, petitioning, and publicity, Connecticut's birth control advocates failed to convince the General Assembly to change the laws. The Connecticut statutes were struck down by the Supreme Court in 1965.)[24]

The majority of former suffrage leaders belonged to the CLWV, which was organized in 1921 by representatives of the CWSA, NWP, Consumers' League, Federation of Colored Women's Clubs, WCTU, League of Nursing, NAACP, League of Republican Women, Democratic Women's Alliance, the Council of Jewish Women, and other groups. They generally retained their LWV memberships through their long public careers. On the other hand, a few former suffragists, such as militant Edna Purtell, disagreed with the League's non-partisan stance. Purtell believed in working for change through the political parties and went on to become active in the Progressive and Democratic parties. "They could write the platforms. They could do the work," she explained in an interview in 1980. Appointed by Democratic governor Wilbur Cross to be a state labor investigator, she led a crusade against child labor in the tobacco fields in the 1930s.[25]

At the time of its founding, leading politicians attacked the CLWV. Republicans accused the women of leaning towards the Democrats; Democrats said they were "too Republican." The influential, pro-Republican Hartford *Courant* warned that women "are forming a new party—a woman's party." The strongest opposition to the CLWV and its program came from politicians—those "whose ox seemed definitely in danger of being gored," as one newspaper so aptly put it. Reportedly referring to League members as "half-baked women" and a "pack of well-fairies," the men who had fought suffrage found CLWV activists "meddlesome." Boss J. Henry Roraback threw Ruth Dadourian out of his office when she asked him for an interview in 1927. As historian Rowland Mitchell has demonstrated, the program of the CLWV was opposed consistently by two highly influential and well organized Connecticut groups, the Chamber of Commerce and the Manufacturers' Association of Connecticut.[26]

The CLWV was founded by sophisticated and experienced

women familiar with the political system and acquainted with many of the state's office holders, party leaders, unionists, and reformers. The CLWV aimed specifically to educate women in government, inspire them to enter politics, and put pressure on legislators to enact social legislation. In the 1920s, the CLWV presented a formal legislative program at every session of the General Assembly. Members testified at hearings, and the organization endorsed such measures as jury duty for women (not passed until 1937), appropriations under the Sheppard-Towner Maternity and Infancy Protection Act of 1921 (denied), aid for handicapped children, shorter hours for women in industry, and other protective legislation. The CLWV launched in 1922 a state-wide campaign of information and open discussion on the reduction of arms. Though few social bills were passed, the League, usually in conjunction with the Consumers' League, persisted. "We never felt hopeless about things, goodness no," recalled Ruth McIntire Dadourian, a League lobbyist and former president who spent more than sixty years in the CLWV. Yet President Mary Bulkley, fearing a decline in membership, warned the women in 1926 not to give up and quit in frustration despite the long-standing opposition to its programs.[27]

With its political education program the CLWV attracted new members to its ranks and introduced them to the structure and functioning of local, state, and national government. In the process, the CLWV became the institution through which many women began their public activity. One such woman was Marian Yeaw Biglow, a Smith College graduate (BA 1911), who had not supported the suffrage movement. "I was opposed to their activities . . . to their method . . . because I did not like this suffragette performance," she recalled in an interview. Moreover, as a young woman, she had "always felt that my menfolk were carrying the load politically . . . . I didn't feel the need for the vote." Nonetheless, when Marian Biglow decided that the local public school was not suitable for her child, she organized a chapter of the CLWV. The women got the town to build a new school, and Biglow went on to work for reform of her local government through the CLWV.[28]

The significance of the CLWV in the post-suffrage era should not be underestimated. It consistently publicized issues of importance to women; encouraged women to register and vote; lobbied for social legislation; promoted international understanding; provided public meetings for candidates to discuss and debate their platforms; carried on a vigorous program of voter education; sent investigators and speakers to state and local institutions, school boards, and city councils; and introduced countless women to public affairs. Dominated by former suffragists who provided guidance and inspiration to younger members, the League became a training ground for politically active women. Many women who later attained public office, including Ella Grasso, the first women in the United States to be elected governor in her own right, were active in the CLWV early in their careers. Grasso considered her work with the CLWV "the best political internship possible for an aspiring politican," and claimed that it gave her "the most detailed and intimate exposure to the workings of local government."[29]

Additional evidence of the vitality of the women's movement after suffrage is the revival of the Connecticut Branch of the NWP in 1922 by Elsie Mary Hill, Josephine Bennett, Katherine Day, and Emily Pierson. Hill, who served as national chairman of the NWP from 1921 until 1925, was a close associate of Alice Paul. In 1922, while attending Yale Law School, she stirred up interest in the NWP. A convention was called in 1922, and the women announced their program, demanding equal employment opportunities for women and the end of special legislation. They believed that a wife should retain her separate identity, that she and her husband should share family headship and family financial burdens, that the law should recognize a woman's property as hers alone, that grounds for divorce should be the same for both parties, that a wife should have an independent choice of citizenship, and that husband and wife should have equal authority over their children. They sought equality before the law and the granting of legal status to homemakers and housekeepers.[30]

The CLWV immediately reacted to the CNWP announcement, carefully noting that it supported parts of the NWP program, but disagreeing with the NWP on special legislation.[31] While ideological differences between the LWV and NWP did exist, it is not evident that the controversy over protective legislation damaged the women's movement in Connecticut, or for that matter, undermined its effectiveness, as historians William O'Neill and William Chafe would have it.[32] The Connecticut Branch of the NWP attracted neither a large following nor wide publicity. Of the original founders, only Hill remained closely identified with the NWP throughout her life, and even she had other interests and organizational ties.

The records show only one occasion in which the controversy

over protective legislation arose in the General Assembly. In 1923, CLWV and Consumers' League lobbyist Mary Welles attacked the NWP for proposing the elimination of legal distinctions between women and men. The speakers were discussing a bill concerning the "moving of boxes, baskets, etc. where women are concerned." Wells criticized State Senator Eugene Goldin for introducing twenty-five bills "to remove the discrimination" between women and men. Those twenty-five bills were rejected along with the bill under consideration. Of course, most social welfare bills were turned down in the 1920s, and the chief opposition did not come from the NWP but from conservative legislators.[33]

Presumably, the public viewed the NWP platform as radical and extreme. Indeed, the NWP program was a dramatic gesture by women committed to social, political, and economic change, and these feminists were promoting the debate of serious social questions. The evidence in Connecticut demonstrates that the passage of so few reforms can hardly be blamed on the NWP, however. As previously noted, the CWSA—"cohesive and committed" and supported by other progressive reformers—had been unable to convince its senators to vote for woman suffrage and its governor to call a special session of the legislature to ratify the suffrage amendment; nor had the united women's movement unseated Senator Brandegee in the 1920 election. The Connecticut experience suggests that even a highly organized and unified feminist movement would not have effected political or social change in the state in the 1920s. The major responsibility for the failure of reform efforts in Connecticut lay with the male politicians and their business and farmer allies.[34]

Perhaps the most dramatic example of the changing political status of Connecticut women in the 1920s was the appearance of female names on election ballots. (Without records of party caucuses or conventions, it is impossible to determine the number of women who expressed interest in running for office or whose names were placed in nomination in the early post-suffrage era. The Connecticut *Register and Manual* gave no statistics on local races and, with the exception of the state House of Representatives, it listed only last names of candidates for other offices. Newspapers occasionally mentioned various women who ran for school boards and other offices, but it is difficult to gather statistics on these elections.)

In 1920, thirty-four women ran for the Connecticut House of Representatives. Of these, twenty-eight ran on the Democratic ticket, three on the Republican, one on the Socialist, one on the

Farmer-Labor, and one as an Independent (though also a nominee of the GOP). Women ran from every county with little if any support from party organizations. In fact, the Democrats were so weak that only thirteen Democrats were elected to the 262-member House that year. The four women who ran as nominees of the Republican party— including Connecticut's only female ordained minister—won! The other successful woman candidate was a Democrat, Helen Jewett of Tolland.[35]

The statistics for the elections of 1922 and 1924 are similar. In 1922, twenty-seven women sought seats in the House; seven were elected, six of whom were Republicans, all from rural sections of the state, and five from GOP strongholds. Of the thirty-four women who ran in 1924, fifteen were elected; *all* were Republicans. Of the forty-seven women elected to state office by 1931 (more than in any other state), forty were Republicans.[36]

Although few of the victors had been prominent suffragists, they directed their campaigns toward women voters. Republican Representative Emily Sophie Brown of Naugatuck claimed interest in aid for children and international relations. A Wellesley graduate, full-time volunteer, and later a member of the CLWV, Brown was elected in 1920. She spoke frequently in committees for social welfare bills during her tenure in office. In the 1921 legislature, Brown and Representative Mary Hooker were instrumental in securing passage of a bill that established the state child welfare bureau. In her campaign, Hooker reminded voters of her support for suffrage and the Consumers' League as well as her concern for prison conditions in the state.[37]

In the 1922 election, women candidates were even more vocal on women's issues. Viola Holt, law student and new Democratic senator from Bristol, pledged to work for legislation protecting women and child workers. During the campaign, Holt commended the Democratic party for "recognizing women distinctly this year." Democratic state Senate candidate, Josepha Whitney, was president of the New Haven League of Women Voters, a peace activist, and a former CWSA officer. She promised the voters, "Everything concerning women and children will be my especial care." Whitney lost the election in 1922 but was elected to the General Assembly in 1932.[38]

Women who attained political office in the early 1920s sometimes credited women for their support. Mary B. Weaver, a farmer and successful candidate for the House in 1922, had been an "ardent" suffragist and was active in the CLWV. She explained her victory: "Women put me in the legislature . . . . The women were wonderful in getting out the vote and a very high percent of the women who were made voters went to the polls. So that the women changed the politics of the town." Emily Sophie Brown, appointed New Haven County Commissioner, later remarked, "The women had a great deal to do with it. Without their hard work and the pressure they brought to bear, [it] would not have been possible." Brown, like many other women of her generation, had a life-long career in social service, working against child labor and pollution of the Naugatuck River, and through the AAUW and CLWV, campaigning to improve penal institutions and public health.[39]

It is difficult to imagine what it was like for a female political candidate in the 1920s. The state was so Republican that one woman, a former suffragist, remarked, "Being a candidate on the Democratic ticket in a hot-bed of Republicans feels extremely uncomfortable and the least said about it the better." The Democrats were more willing to nominate women, but the party was too weak to win elections. A few women ran on third party tickets. Josephine Bennett, militant suffragist and the "fearless and joyful politician of the radicals," ran for the United States Senate on the Farmer-Labor ticket in 1920 and for Attorney-General of Connecticut in 1922 on the Socialist/Farmer-Labor ticket; Elsie Hill ran for Secretary of the State as a nominee of the Farmer-Labor party in 1920 and later, as an Independent Republican, for the General Assembly and the United States Congress. Mary Dworkin of Bridgeport was a nominee of the radical Workers' party in 1922. All lost by wide margins. This is not surprising since Republicans were so entrenched and radical ideas were suspect in the post-war period.[40]

Nominations by the GOP, on the other hand, were a virtual guarantee of victory in many parts of the state. Edith Valet Cook, elected in 1926 to the House, reminisced on her campaign: "It was almost a foregone conclusion at that time. You were nominated as a Republican, and everyone was a Republican, so you got elected." Helen A. Green recalled that she was a "good worker" for the Republican party once she had registered in 1920. She was nominated for the General Assembly in 1924. She spoke about her election in a 1980 interview: "In those years, Granby was a big Republican town. You didn't have to worry. Once you got the nomination in the caucus, that was it."[41]

Seats in the General Assembly frequently were viewed by the party in power as a form of patronage and were passed around to party loyalists who rarely were in office long enough to move into the ranks of leadership. Yet such independent, reform-minded women as Cook, Corinne Alsop, Emily Sophie Brown, and others served in the legislature during the 1920s. These women often supported measures opposed by the Republican party. "Oh, I probably was asked to vote for a bill or two," recalled Edith Valet Cook, "but if I didn't want to, I didn't." Alsop remained an outspoken critic of Roraback throughout her career in politics. Though usually put on the least powerful committees, e.g., Humane Institutions, State Library, Public Health and Safety, women legislators became strong backers of such bills as those to provide an eight-hour day for children, ratification of the national child labor amendment (it failed twice), and more women factory inspectors.[42]

Also significant was the decision by women legislators to set up an organization aimed "to help one another learn 'where to go, what to do, and whom to see' " in the General Assembly. Under the leadership of Julia Emery of Stamford, they formed the Connecticut Order of Women Legislators in 1927 and the National OWLs in 1938 to educate women serving in state legislatures on governmental matters and political procedures and to assist women who were seeking public office.[43]

Beyond the extension of the franchise, it is difficult to measure changes in the political status of women in the 1920s. No Connecticut women attained high political office in the state or national government. Yet, a substantial number sought and were elected to office. Of the forty-seven women who held seats in the state legislature by 1931, nineteen served more than one term. Many more women received political appointments to local and state commissions and boards. During a period of conservative rule and suspicion of progressive ideas, they kept alive issues that had concerned women for generations. Suffragists still dominated the CLWV and other pressure groups, but in the 1920s other women joined these organizations and began public careers.

Many factors beyond feminists' control account for the inability of female reformers to effect the changes which they had envisioned. The national mood was conservative. Moreover, the state experienced a serious economic decline in the post-war period. The GOP leadership and most members of the General Assembly were unsympathetic to economic, political, or social reform. Because of continued malapportionment, those for whom much social legislation was intended—the urban workers—had little voice in their government. As historian Rowland Mitchell has noted: "Wage earners as a group were not represented among the voting population in proportion to their actual numbers. Because of this political parties could more safely disregard the wage-eners as a special group."[44]

Lawmakers not only felt no compulsion to win favor with urban voters, but also were committed to a tax system which favored business. Property taxes were the major source of income; corporate taxes remained low and no personal income tax was enacted. The Democratic party did make gestures toward urban wage-earners, but because of its weak organization and its indifference to the recruitment of new immigrants, its representation in the General Assembly remained small.[45]

In the last year of the suffrage movement, suffragists pursued tactics which allowed the men in power to weaken the potential of the women's movement in subsequent elections. By making endorsement of suffrage the major campaign issue of 1920, they provided an opportunity for long-time opponents to get on the "pro" side. Thus, candidates who only belatedly came out for ratification could campaign as supporters of the amendment. Then, to assure large numbers of female registrants, the CWSA supported party efforts to register new voters. The GOP welcomed this opportunity and actively recruited women members.

At this stage, the GOP had everything to gain and nothing to lose by swinging to the pro-suffrage camp. Connecticut had been only the thirty-seventh state to ratify. Women presumably would have voted in November without Connecticut's ratification. Moreover, once registered as Republicans, women were more likely to be persuaded to demonstrate party loyalty by voting the straight ticket.

In a study of pacifist women's activities in the 1920s, historian Joan M. Jensen has concluded that "organized women . . . were not 'weak sisters' unable to work together but . . . powerful women who provoked strong reactions by their bid for political power." The Connecticut example supports this analysis. In pursuing their political goals, Connecticut feminists faced opposition so formidable that they were unable to achieve their aims through the channels traditionally available to men. For example, the politicians who controlled the machine refused to grant women decision-making roles on their party committees. They gave official status to more conservative women—those who had never been active suffragists or even leading anti-suffragists.[46]

Nonetheless, former suffrage leaders did not withdraw from political activism in the post-suffrage era. Using the tactics of pre-suffrage days—publicity, lobbying, letter-writing, and political education—they continued to advocate social welfare legislation, international cooperation, and the extension of women's rights. Throughout the period of this study, increasing numbers of women became involved in local and state politics through party work and particularly through the CLWV where they became familiar with the political process and gained valuable experience which would benefit them and others new to politics in the following decades.

American women in 1920 were enthusiastic about the opportunity for change which their enfranchisement represented. If the women's movement failed to achieve its goals of a more just and humane society, it was mainly because women did not participate as equals in their government. The right to vote did not open the doors to the "smoke-filled rooms" where nominations, appointments, and platforms were decided. As long as politicians could operate without regard for the needs and desires of the citizenry, women were compelled to work for change mostly in pressure groups outside of the traditional party structure. This they continued to do in Connecticut after 1920.

NOTES

I would like to thank Alice Miller, Judith Papachristou, and George Nichols for their helpful comments and suggestions during the course of this project. I deeply appreciate the advice and encouragement which Gerda Lerner has provided since the beginning of my research on Connecticut women. For their understanding and moral support, I am most grateful to my family.

Introduction

1. I have examined the Connecticut documents in light of generalizations by those historians whose work has been particularly influential in interpreting the women's movement of the early twentieth century. These include: Eleanor Flexner, *Century of Struggle* (New York, 1959); Aileen Kraditor, *The Ideas of the Woman Suffrage Movement, 1890-1920* (Garden City, 1965); William O'Neill, *Everyone Was Brave* (New York, 1969) and *The Woman Movement* (Chicago, 1969); Alan Grimes, *The Puritan Ethic and Woman Suffrage* (New York, 1967); William H. Chafe, *The American Woman* (London, 1972); and Carl Degler, *At Odds: Women and the Family in America from the Revolution to the Present* (New York, 1980).

On the history of the woman suffrage movement, see also Ellen Carol DuBois, *Feminism and Suffrage* (Ithaca, 1978); David Morgan, *Suffragists and Democrats* (East Lansing, 1972); Ross Evans Paulson, *Women's Suffrage and Prohibition: A Comparative Study of Equality and Social Control* (Glenview, Illinois, 1973); Anne F. Scott and Andrew M. Scott, *One Half the People: The Fight for Woman Suffrage* (Philadelphia, 1975); and Andrew Sinclair, *The Better Half: The Emancipation of the American Woman* (New York, 1965).

The participants themselves wrote valuable histories of the suffrage movement. The most important is the *History of Woman Suffrage* (hereafter *HWS*), 6 vols., edited by Elizabeth Cady Stanton, Matilda J. Gage, Ida H. Harper, and Susan B. Anthony (New York, 1886-1922); see also Carrie Chapman Catt and Nettie Rogers Shuler, *Woman Suffrage and Politics* (New York, 1923); Inez Haynes Irwin, *Angels and Amazons* (Garden City, 1923) and *The Story of the Woman's Party* (New York, 1921); Maud Wood Park, *Front Door Lobby* (Boston, 1960); and Doris Stevens, *Jailed For Freedom* (New York, 1976).

With respect to the question of the impact of woman suffrage on American politics and the "failure" of the feminist movement, see, for example, O'Neill, *Woman Movement*, in which the author asserts that enfranchisement was "the most dramatic accomplishment" of the early twentieth-century women's movement (p. 93), and, indeed, marked "not . . . the beginning of women's real emancipation, but its end. While hardly anyone could see this in 1920, by 1930 it was patently obvious" (p. 88). See the chapter in *Woman Movement*, "The End of Feminism," pp. 89-97, in which O'Neill discusses the failure of woman suffrage to initiate "sweeping social reforms" (p. 89) and to launch a new generation of enfranchised women into careers in public life. See also O'Neill's chapter, "The Post-Suffrage Era" in *Everyone Was Brave*, pp. 264-294.

While she acknowledged that an "enormous change took place with the enactment of the Nineteenth Amendment," Kraditor, in *Ideas,* characterizes that change as no more than a feeling on the part of suffragists "of new pride in American democracy and a new respect for themselves" (p. 218). Noting also that "the addition of women to the electorate has not significantly altered American voting patterns" (p. 218), she also points out that "suffragists overestimated what they could accomplish with the vote" (p. 49).

Like O'Neill and Kraditor, Chafe in the *American Woman*, has emphasized the gap between the "inflated rhetoric of female leaders" (p. 45) and the paucity of reforms actually accomplished by the vote. In Chafe's view, "women's political standing plummeted" during the post-suffrage era because women were unable to organize sufficiently to force politicians to act in favor of their programs (pp. 29-30). Moreover, they continued "to follow . . . the lead of their husbands and fathers in the world outside the home." Thus, according to Chafe, the "reform meant relatively little" (p. 246).

O'Neill also has stressed the failure of a women's vote to emerge after 1920, concluding that "once the women's vote was shown to be a 'paper tiger,' female organizations often carried less weight with professional politicians than before." *Woman Movement,* pp. 92-93.

Degler's interpretation of suffrage and its aftermath summarizes such views:

> Though the suffrage cause in the 19th century became increasingly central to the feminist cause, suffrage, once achieved, had almost no observable effect upon the position of women. To listen to the advocates of woman suffrage . . . one would have thought that the millenium would result once women were permitted to vote . . . . Of course none of these things happened. In fact . . . women did not even make as much use of the ballot as expected, much less bring about any significant social or economic changes." (*At Odds,* p. 328)

A fundamental aspect of the suffrage movement, not explored by any of these historians, has been discussed by Ellen Carol Dubois, who concluded that suffragism was

> the first independent movement of women for their own liberation. Its growth—the mobilization of women around the demand for the vote, their collective activity, their

commitment to gaining increased power over their own lives—was itself a major change in the condition of those lives. (*Feminism and Suffrage,* pp. 17-18)

2. Carol Ruth Berkin has noted the tendency of historians toward a "merciless dissection of the [women's] movement" which has resulted in the "isolation of a social movement from the larger context in which, perforce, it operated, and an internal exploration that seriously distorts the complex relationship between the women's movement and American society." Berkin suggests that in "laying the blame for the unfinished revolution on their shoulders, historians have invested these women with the very control over events and over their own destinies that they had long been seeking." She reminds us, however, that in the 1920s there were "concrete signs that the social and political milieu in which they operated as a minority was hostile to further reform." Indeed, she adds, "open hostility to reform groups grew during the postwar era, and feminism, like labor organizations, was labeled foreign, dangerous, un-American." See "Not Separate, Not Equal" in *Women of America: A History,* by Carol Ruth Berkin and Mary Beth Norton (Boston, 1979), pp. 273 and 275.

3. Flexner, Kraditor, and O'Neill have stressed the conservative nature of the leadership and ideology of the woman suffrage movement, particularly in its later years. Flexner noted a "steady trend . . . toward the conservative and conventional" (p. 217) and concluded that the middle-class perspective of the leadership and rank-and-file suffragists was too limited to draw poor and working women to the struggle (p. 247). See *Century of Struggle.*

Kraditor argued that the "vast majority" of suffragists sought merely to participate "more fully in the affairs of a government the basic structure of which they accepted" (*Ideas,* pp. 25-26). She believed that most women were drawn to the suffrage cause only to achieve the vote and not because they had an ideological commitment to an egalitarian society or a genuine desire to bring about social, political, or economic change. See *Ideas,* pp. 105-137.

In *Woman Movement,* O'Neill claimed that women joined the "woman movement" more out of "intelligent self-interest" (p. 42) than because of a clearly definable and rational vision of a just society. He believed that the majority of reform-minded activists, "social feminists," were seeking to relieve personal frustrations rather than to effect change: highly educated with few occupational choices, they found themselves a "functionless elite" (p. 45) without the female "camaraderie" (p. 57) of their school days. Women's organizations, he concluded, were "safety valves by which frustrated women could find an outlet for talents and ambitions that home life could neither satisfy nor healthily contain" (p. 43). O'Neill criticized what he considered the women's lack of understanding of the political and economic realities of their time and their naive expectations of a transformation of American society once the vote was won (p. 70). The post-suffrage era did not mark the beginning of a new period of reform, because, according to O'Neill, women did not develop an ideology (i.e., socialism) that would cross class lines and convince women to vote as a bloc. If women "had been wiser and more daring, they would have come closer to building the good society of their dreams" (p. 97). See also *Everyone Was Brave,* p. 143, and Degler, *At Odds,* pp. 334-336.

According to Chafe, feminism waned and social legislation was not passed because "the mass of female citizens failed to act in the cohesive and committed manner which the suffragists had predicted" (*American Woman,* pp. 29-30). Chafe noted, rightly, that enfranchisement alone could not alter sexual inequality. He argued that the socialization process encouraged women to accept their subordinate status; that "only a substantial upheaval could modify the existing division of labor between the sexes"; and that World War II was that upheaval. See pp. 246-247.

According to Alan Grimes, woman suffrage was part of an effort by conservative politicians to counterbalance urban immigrant votes by increasing the number of middle-class, Protestant, native-born, rural voters (*Puritan Ethic,* p. 118). Kraditor believes that many suffragists willingly compromised their democratic principles to "find a favorable hearing from the men from whom they sought their political liberty" (*Ideas,* p. 44). The nativist strain in suffrage arguments has been noted also by Chafe, *American Woman,* p. 15, and O'Neill, *Everyone Was Brave,* pp. 7-75.

    4. On divisions in the women's movement during the suffrage struggle, see for example, Flexner, *Century of Struggle,* pp. 173-175; O'Neill, *Woman Movement,* pp. 76-80; and Janice Law Trecker in Stevens, *Jailed For Freedom,* pp. v-xxxi.

    On divisions in the post-suffrage era, see O'Neill, *Woman Movement,* pp. 90-93, and *Everyone Was Brave,* pp. 274-294; Chafe, *American Woman,* pp. 112-132; and Degler, *At Odds,* pp. 359-361.

    5. In his discussion of the post-suffrage era, O'Neill implies that women did not want public roles. Commenting on the difficulties which women continued to face when they tried to combine marriage, family, and work outside the home, O'Neill concludes: "Under the circumstances, women could hardly be blamed for declining public roles that brought them few rewards and many hardships." *Woman Movement,* p. 94. According to Chafe, "it became increasingly clear . . . that enthusiasm among females for reform was limited at best" (*American Woman,* p. 30).

    6. Much of the six-volume *History of Woman Suffrage* is a compilation of reports of state activities.

    7. On the movement for a federal amendment, see, for example, Flexner, *Century of Struggle,* pp. 173-175, and Scott and Scott, *One Half the People,* pp. 31-37.

    8. These activities have been discussed in J. Stanley Lemons, *The Woman Citizen* (Urbana, 1973), and Clarke A. Chambers, *Seedtime of Reform: American Social Service and Social Action, 1918-1933* (Minneapolis, 1963). Also see below, Chapter 3.

    9. An exception to the "national perspective" on suffrage is Sharon Hartman Strom's "Leadership and Tactics in the American Woman Suffrage Movement: A New Pespective from Massachusetts," *Journal of American History,* vol. 62, no. 2 (September, 1975), 296-315. Strom has demonstrated that the emphasis of the "national" histories on Massachusetts as the center of the conservative wing of the movement, has distorted the picture of the struggle in that state and failed to notice the vigorous activity which led to a strong battle for a suffrage referendum in 1915 and to early ratification of the Nineteenth Amendment in 1919.

    A recent study of suffrage and its aftermath on the state level is Joan M. Jensen, " 'Disfranchisement is a Disgrace': Women and Politics in New Mexico, 1900-1940," *New Mexico Historical Review,* vol. 56, no. 1 (Jan., 1981), 5-35.

    10. In the *Woman Citizen,* Lemons has provided one of the few accounts of the post-suffrage era which demonstrates women's continuing commitment to reform in the 1920s. He has argued that women's reform organizations provided the ideological link between Progressivism and the New Deal. See pp. vii-ix.

    11. Ruth McIntire Dadourian, "Connecticut Has Most Women Legislators," *Hartford Daily Times,* Jan. 20, 1927, p. 1, in possession of R. M. Dadourian.

    12. A recent oral history project, "The Political Activities of the First Generation of Fully Enfranchised Connecticut Women," contains interviews conducted by Carole Nichols and Joyce Pendery with twenty-one women active in Connecticut political life between 1915 and 1945. The group includes organization leaders, party workers, and office holders. These interviews provide ample evidence of women's varied activities during the period. Transcripts at University of Connecticut, Storrs; Connecticut Humanities Resource Center, New Haven; and Connecticut State Library, Hartford.

    13. On Connecticut's "New Deal," see Albert E. Van Dusen, *Connecticut* (New York, 1961), pp. 291-314.

    14. Eleanor H. Little, interview, June 11, 1980, transcript at University of Connecticut, Storrs. On women who began their public careers in their own communities, see also interviews with Helen Binney Kitchel, Edna Mary Purtell, Hazel Thrall Sullivan, Percy Maxim Lee, and Chase Going Woodhouse, transcripts at University of Connecticut, Storrs.

    For names of office-holders, see *Connecticut Register and Manual,* published annually by the State of Connecticut (Hartford).

Susan Ware has offered a portrait of the women who played important roles in the planning and administration of New Deal programs. She has noted that many of these women shared "common experiences in the woman suffrage campaign." *Beyond Suffrage: Women in the New Deal* (Cambridge, Massachusetts, 1981), pp. 1-2.

Chapter One

1. The history of the Connecticut Woman Suffrage Association can be traced through the following documents: Papers of the Connecticut Woman Suffrage Association, 1869-1921 (hereafter CWSA Papers), Connecticut State Library, Hartford; Records of the National Woman Suffrage Association (hereafter NAWSA Records), Library of Congress; and the Papers of the National Woman's Party (hereafter NWP Papers), Library of Congress. Also useful are the sections on Connecticut in *HWS*, III, pp. 316-338; *HWS*, IV, pp. 535-542; and *HWS*, VI, pp. 68-85.
2. *HWS*, IV, pp. 535-542. On Connecticut politics in the first decades of the twentieth century, see Van Dusen, *Connecticut*; Ruth O. M. Anderson, *From Yankee to American: Connecticut 1865-1914* (Chester, Connecticut, 1975); Lane W. Lancaster, "Background of a State Boss System," *American Journal of Sociology*, 35 (1930), 783-798; Lane W. Lancaster, "The Democratic Party in Connecticut," *National Municipal Review*, 17 (Aug., 1928), 451-455; and Lane W. Lancaster, "Rotten Boroughs and the Connecticut Legislature," *National Municipal Review*, 13 (Dec., 1924), 678-683.
3. *HWS*, III, pp. 319-335. Burr later was part of a group of twenty-three women comprising the "Revising Committee" which published Part I of the *Woman's Bible* in 1895. She was one of eight women who wrote special commentaries in the book. See Kraditor, *Ideas*, p. 67, notes 8 and 9, p. 77.
4. *HWS*, III, pp. 320-328. For a short portrait of Isabella Beecher Hooker, see Ann Farnum, "Woman Suffrage As An Alternative to the Beecher Ministry: The Conversion of Isabella Beecher Hooker," *Portraits of a Nineteenth Century Family*, ed. by Earl A. French and Diana Royce (Hartford, 1976), pp. 69-97.
5. *HWS*, III, pp. 321, 335, and 324. Both Catherine Beecher and Harriet Beecher Stowe later withdrew their support for woman suffrage. See Farnum, *ibid*.
6. *Ibid.*, pp. 321-322. Numerous tracts and memoranda issued by the CWSA testify to the breadth of their program. See CWSA Papers and NAWSA Records, containers 8, 14, 48, 49, 51, 52, and 67.
7. See, for example, *HWS*, III, p. 338; *HWS*, IV, pp. 535-539; and CWSA Minute Books, 1869-1920, 3 vols., in CWSA Papers. On the Smith sisters, see *HWS*, III, pp. 328-330; the quote is from the *Hartford Times* (1878) in *HWS*, III, p. 329.
8. *HWS*, IV, pp. 537-542; *HWS*, VI, p. 83; and Anderson, *From Yankee to American*, pp. 22-23.
9. Degler, *At Odds*, pp. 356-357.
10. *HWS*, IV, pp. 539-541.
11. *Ibid.*, p. 537. Also see below, chapter 3.
12. *HWS*, IV, pp. 539-542.
13. CWSA, Executive Board Meeting (hereafter EBM), April 15, 1918, CWSA Papers and NAWSA Records, cont. 51; Josephine B. Bennett to Mabel Vernon, April 4, 1918, NWP Papers, tray 17.
14. *HWS*, IV, pp. 541-542.
15. *Ibid.*, pp. 536-542.
16. *Ibid.*, Anderson, *From Yankee to American*, pp. 22-24; Janice Law Trecker, *Preachers, Rebels, and Traders: Connecticut 1818-1865* (Chester, Connecticut, 1975), p. 3; Van Dusen, *Connecticut*, pp. 210 and 254-256.
17. *HWS*, IV, p. 536.
18. *HWS*, VI, p. 69; CWSA Convention, Meriden, Connecticut, Nov. 2, 1906, in CWSA Minute Books, vol. 2, pp. 194-199, CWSA Papers.

19. Anderson, *From Yankee to American,* pp. 2, 28-30; Van Dusen, *Connecticut,* p. 264; Lancaster, "Background," p. 793; and Rowland Mitchell, Jr., "Social Legislation in Connecticut, 1919-1939" (unpublished PhD dissertation, Yale University, 1954), pp. 7-17.

20. *HWS,* IV, pp. 536-542; see also CWSA Papers. A special state-wide election in November, 1901, indicated a popular demand for a constitutional convention to alter the representation in the Assembly. Like the General Assembly it was supposed to reapportion, the convention had an overrepresentation of rural towns. The resulting constitution differed only slightly from the original. Five times during the four-month meeting, a woman suffrage resolution was submitted to the representatives, and each time it failed. The citizens of the state rejected the entire document, however, and Connecticut retained its 1818 Constitution until 1965. See Anderson, *From Yankee to American,* pp. 27-28.

21. Samuel Koenig, "Ethnic Factors in the Economic Life of Urban Connecticut," *American Sociological Review,* 8 (April, 1943), p. 197.

22. Lancaster, "Rotten Boroughs," p. 680; David M. Roth, *Connecticut* (New York, 1979), pp. 162-173; Van Dusen, *Connecticut,* pp. 261-263.

23. Lancaster, "Rotten Boroughs," p. 681, and "Democratic Party," p. 453; Anderson, *From Yankee to American,* pp. 29-30; Mitchell, "Social Legislation," p. 125. On a brief alliance between unionists and Democrats at the turn of the century, see Frederick M. Heath, "Labor and the Progressive Movement in Connecticut," *Labor History,* 12 (Winter, 1971), pp. 65-67.

24. Anderson, *From Yankee to American,* pp.30-33; Roth, *Connecticut,* p. 173; Van Dusen, *Connecticut,* pp. 262-263. Republican Joseph W. Alsop led the state's efforts to elect former President and Progressive Theodore Roosevelt in 1912. Alsop was a wealthy tobacco farmer and merchant, President of the Tobacco Growers Association, and a rival of state Republican boss J. Henry Roraback. Alsop's wife, Corinne Robinson Alsop, was a niece of Roosevelt. She later became an active suffragist and politician. See Anderson, *From Yankee to American,* pp. 29-33; and Durward Howes, ed., *American Women: The Standard Biographical Dictionary of Notable Women,* Vol. III, 1939-1940 (3 Vols., Los Angeles, 1935-1939), p. 17.

The Republicans controlled the Connecticut House of Representatives through the 1940s and the Senate until 1933. For composition of the General Assembly, consult the *Connecticut Register and Manual* for appropriate years.

25. Mitchell, "Social Legislation," pp. 78, 87-88, and 122-123; Lancaster, "Democratic Party," p. 454; Van Dusen, *Connecticut,* pp. 285-286; CWSA, "The Republican Machine in 1919-1920," NAWSA Records, cont. 51; Lancaster, "Background," pp. 796-797. Favorable legislation made it possible for the Connecticut Light and Power Company to expand continuously until that utility dominated the state. Roraback became president of the multi-million-dollar operation in 1920 while chairman of the Republican State Central Committee: See Herbert F. Janick, Jr., *A Diverse People: Connecticut 1914 to the Present* (Chester, Connecticut, 1975), p. 26. On the conservative press, see also Ruth McIntire Dadourian, interview, June 30, 1980, transcript at University of Connecticut, Storrs. On Roraback and Republican dominance of Connecticut politics, see Edwin Dahill, "Connecticut's J. Henry Roraback" (unpublished Ph.D. dissertation, Teachers College, Columbia University, 1971).

26. Lancaster, "Background," p. 793; Mitchell, "Social Legislation," pp. 21-23.

27. Maud Hincks to Alice Stone Blackwell, May 17, 1913, NAWSA Records, cont. 8. See also Roth, *Connecticut,* pp. 153-157.

28. Examples of suffrage rhetoric are found in "Public Hearings Before the Joint Standing Committee on Woman Suffrage," Connecticut General Assembly, 1917 and 1919, and "Public Hearings Before the Joint Standing Committee on the Judidiary," 1917, Connecticut State Library, Hartford; see also CWSA Papers and NAWSA Records. On this new group of suffragists, see *HWS,* VI, pp. 68-73; and Annie G. Porritt, *Bridgeport Herald* (hereafter *BH*), November 7, 1920, p. 19.

29. Porritt, *BH,* Nov. 7, 1920, p. 19.

30. On Ruutz-Rees: *Biographical Cyclopaedia of American Women* (New York, 1924),

pp. 180–181; Howes, *American Women, 1939–1940,* p. 783; John William Leonard, ed., *Woman's Who's Who of America, 1914–1915* (New York, 1914, republished, 1976), p. 709. On Seton: CWSA *News Bulletin,* Oct. 20, 1917, NAWSA Records, cont. 51; Porritt, *BH,* Nov. 7, 1920, p. 19, and Jan. 9, 1921, p. 9; Howes, *American Women, 1939–1940,* p. 810; Leonard, *Woman's Who's Who,* p. 730; Joan Feinberg, "Grace Gallatin Seton," in Barbara Sicherman and Carol Hurd Green, eds., *Notable American Women: The Modern Period* (Cambridge, MA, 1980), pp. 639–641.

On Parker: Leonard, *Woman's Who's Who,* p. 622; Connecticut General Assembly, "Hearings . . . on Humane Institutions," 1917 and 1919, and "Hearings . . . on Labor," 1921.

31. On Pierson: Katharine Houghton Hepburn to Alice Paul, Sept. 12, 1917, NWP Papers; Porritt, *BH,* Nov. 7, 1920, p. 19; Leonard, *Woman's Who's Who,* p. 647; *HWS,* VI, p. 70.

32. On Hepburn: John A. Garraty, ed., *Dictionary of American Biography,* Supplement Five, 1951-1955 (New York, 1977), pp. 296-297; Leonard, *Woman's Who's Who,* p. 382; Porritt, *BH,* Nov. 7, 1920, p. 19; References to the report on prostitution are in a letter from Katharine Houghton Hepburn to Miss [Agnes] Ryan of the *Woman's Journal,* Sept. 22, 1913, NAWSA Records, cont. 8.

33. *HWS,* VI, pp. 68–73; See also Porritt, *BH,* Nov. 7, 1920, p. 19.

34. Porritt, *BH,* Nov. 7, 1920, p. 19; *HWS,* VI, pp. 68–73; CWSA, "To the Members of the House of Representatives: A Presentation," 1911, in Connecticut State Library; Emily Pierson claimed 32,000 members in a memorandum discussing the 1917 Judiciary hearings, Feb. 27, 1917, in CWSA Papers.

35. I have not been able to determine the number of women who belonged to the suffrage associations in 1920. The number of top leaders is approximate. It is likely that other women had equally influential positions in the associations. I have used the following criteria for selection of the twenty-nine women. Each woman fits into at least two of the three categories: (a) They were singled out as prominent leaders in suffrage literature; (b) Their activities were highly visible; their names turned up frequently in the documents and in newspapers; (c) They held high offices or headed important committees in the organizations.

36. At least twelve women were on the payrolls of the two suffrage groups between 1917 and 1920. This number includes only those whose employment or salary was noted specifically in minutes of meetings or in correspondence. The expenses of many workers also were paid at times. See NAWSA Records and CWSA Papers; on worker's support for suffrage, see below, Chapter two.

37. Lemons, *Woman Citizen,* p. 111; Leonard, *Woman's Who's Who,* p. 250; James P. Louis, "Josephine Marshall Jewell Dodge" in Edward T. James, ed., *Notable American Women, 1607–1950,* 3 vols. (Cambridge, MA, 1971), I, p. 492; Flexner, *Century of Struggle,* p. 296; *Connecticut Register and Manual* (1979), p. 91; *HWS,* III, p. 335; VI, p. 85; and Lillian Ascough to Anne Martin, Feb. 14–18, 1918, NWP Papers, tray 14.

38. "Hearings . . . on the Judiciary," 1917, pp. 33–34; "Hearings . . . on Woman Suffrage," 1919, pp. 6–21; *BH,* Dec. 5, 1920, p. 19; Dec. 19, 1920, pp. 1 and 9; Jan. 2, 1921, p. 19; Jan. 19, 1921, p. 1; Hartford *Courant,* Jan. 1, 1921, p. 3; Lemons, *Woman Citizen,* p. 111.

39. CWSA, *News from Suffrage Headquarters,* Jan. 12, 1917, NAWSA Records, cont. 52.

40. On groups visited, see, for example: "List of organizations visited by NWP workers," 1917, NWP Papers, tray 14; Katherine M. Mullen and Catherine M. Flanagan, "Report of Organizers for Feb. 1st to 15th, 1918," NWP Papers, tray 17; CWSA EBM, May 15, 1918, CWSA Papers; CWSA EBM, July 17, 1918, NAWSA Records, cont. 51. On suffrage arguments, see "Hearings . . . on Woman Suffrage," 1917 and 1919.

41. "Proceedings of the Connecticut Federation of Labor," 1917, resolutions 6, 7, 11, 13, pp. 8–9; CWSA *News from Suffrage Headquarters,* Jan. 12, 1917, NAWSA Records, cont. 52; *BH,* Sept. 18, 1918, p. 3; *Hartford Courant,* Sept. 5, 1918, p. 2; CWSA EBM,

Oct. 9, 1918, NAWSA Records, cont. 51; *Bridgeport Times,* Jan. 22, 1919, p. 7; Janick, *Diverse People,* pp. 33-35.

42. On suffrage and the war: see Chafe, *American Woman,* pp. 48-55; O'Neill, *Woman Movement,* pp. 78-81; Flexner, *Century of Struggle,* pp. 283-293. Involvement of Connecticut women: Papers of the Connecticut State Council of Defense, Women's Division, Connecticut State Library, Hartford; Feinberg, "Grace Gallatin Seton," Sicherman and Green, *Notable American Women: The Modern Period,* pp. 639-641. CWSA leader and president of the New Haven Equal Franchise League (1915-1918), Josepha Whitney, was chairman of the Connecticut chapter of the Woman's Peace Party when the United States entered the war. In order to avoid anti-suffragist attacks on suffragists as pacifists, Whitney resigned from the Peace Party and was active in CWSA war work. She became active in the peace movement after 1920. See Herbert Janick, "An Instructive Failure: The Connecticut Peace Movement, 1919-1939," *Peace and Change,* 5 (Spring, 1978), p. 13.

43. CWSA Central Committee on War Work, "Preliminary Statement," (n.d.), NAWSA Records, cont. 51; CWSA *News Bulletin,* Sept. 18, 1917, NAWSA Records, cont. 51.

44. "Preliminary Statement," NAWSA Records, cont. 51. On the Bridgeport War Workers, see Amy Hewes, *Women as Munitions Makers* (New York, 1917); and Esther Norton, "Women in War Industries," *The New Republic* (Dec. 15, 1917), pp. 179-182.

45. Josephine B. Bennett to Executive Board of the CWSA, Aug. 31, 1917, NAWSA Records, cont. 51; O'Neill, *Woman Movement,* pp. 78-81; Flexner, *Century of Struggle,* pp. 283-293; *HWS,* VI, p. 73; Porritt, *BH,* Nov. 7, 1920, p. 19.

46. Flexner, *Century of Struggle,* p. 173-175; Scott and Scott, *One Half the People,* pp. 31-37; O'Neill, *Woman Movement,* pp. 76-80; Kraditor, *Ideas,* pp. 192-194; Trecker in Stevens, *Jailed For Freedom,* pp. v-xxi.

47. Katharine H. Hepburn to Mrs. Gardener, Jan. 27, 1914, and Feb. 9, 1914; Katharine H. Hepburn to Mrs. Medill McCormick, Jan. 22, 1914, and Feb. 5, 1914; Katherine B. Day and Annie Porritt to Carrie Chapman Catt, May 29, 1915, NAWSA Records, cont. 48. See also Stevens, *Jailed For Freedom,* p. 361; Annie G. Porritt to Anne Martin, Jan. 15, 1917, NWP Papers, tray 14; *BH,* Nov. 7, 1920, p. 19.

48. Flexner, *Century of Struggle,* pp. 283-284.

49. Stevens, *Jailed For Freedom,* pp. 354-371; Dorothy J. Bartlett to Catherine Flanagan, Nov. 30, 1917, NWP Papers, tray 14. The "Picketing" trays (47 and 48) of the NWP Papers contain prison documents, including numerous statements and letters from prisoners. From released prisoners, the NWP collected affidavits, describing conditions in the Occoquan Workhouse and Old District Jail, where the women were detained. Included are affidavits by Dorothy Bartlett and Valeria Parker, M.D., who visited Bartlett in prison.

Two letters of resignation are among the documents: Katharine H. Hepburn to the Executive Board of the CWSA, Sept. 19, 1917, CWSA Papers; Josephine B. Bennett to the Executive Board of the CWSA, Aug. 31, 1917, NAWSA Records, cont. 51. See also *HWS,* VI, p. 74.

50. Katharine H. Hepburn to Alice Paul, Sept. 26, 1917, NWP Papers, tray 14; Katharine H. Hepburn to Executive Board of the CWSA, Sept. 19, 1917, CWSA Papers; CWSA *News Bulletin,* Oct. 20, 1917, NAWSA Records, cont. 51; CWSA *News Bulletin,* Nov. 14, 1917, NAWSA Records, cont. 51.

51. CWSA *News Bulletin,* Sept. 20, 1917, NAWSA Records, cont. 51; Minutes of EBMs of the CWSA, 1917-1920 for examples of Hepburn's attendance, CWSA Papers; Katharine H. Hepburn to Alice Paul, Sept. 26, 1917, NWP Papers, tray 14.

52. On Ludington's background, see Howes, *American Women, 1939-1940,* p. 19; and the *New York Times* (hereafter *NYT*), March 3, 1953, p. 29, and March 21, 1953, p. 16. Her statement on taking office is in the CWSA *News Bulletin,* Oct. 20, 1917, NAWSA Records, cont. 51; see also CWSA *News Bulletin,* Sept. 18 and Nov. 14, 1917; and *BH,* Nov. 7, 1920, p. 19, Nov. 21, 1920, p. 19, and Dec. 19, 1920, p. 8. For reminiscences on Ludington, see Dadourian, interview, June 30, 1980, pp. 17-18.

60   VOTES AND MORE FOR WOMEN

The CWSA did not abandon entirely its effort to gain the vote by state legislation, and suffrage bills were proposed and supported in 1917 and 1919. Nonetheless, Ludington and the Executive Board said that they wanted "to avoid the expense and work of a State campaign, when the gaining of full suffrage by Federal Amendment is a matter of such a short time." Katharine Ludington, "Important" (n.d.), NAWSA Records, cont. 51; see also CWSA EBM, Jan. 22, 1919, CWSA Papers.

53. Catherine Flanagan to Alice Paul, Feb. 5, 1918, NWP Papers, tray 17; Annie G. Porritt to Maud Younger, Aug. 9, 1919, NWP Papers, tray 19. See also Catherine Flanagan to Rosamond Danielson, Dec. 22, 1917, NAWSA Records, cont. 51.

Examples of friction between CWSA and NWP include: CWSA EBM, Oct. 9, 1918, NAWSA Records, cont. 51; Annie G. Porritt to Anne Martin, Jan. 15, 1917, NWP Papers, tray 14; Lillian Ascough to Alice Paul, Aug. 20, 1917, NWP Papers, tray 14. Evidence of friction *within* the NWP includes: Josephine Bennett to Alice Paul, Jan. 31, 1919, NWP Papers, tray 20; Helena Hill Weed to Alice Paul, April 5 and April 6, 1920, NWP Papers, tray 23.

54. Dadourian, interview, June 30, 1980, p. 21. Hepburn wrote to Alice Paul about the CWSA work in the state: Katharine Houghton Hepburn to Alice Paul, Feb. 27, 1920, NWP Papers, tray 23.

55. Daphne Selden used the term "extremists" in a letter to Rosamond Danielson, Jan. 8, 1918, NAWSA Records, cont. 51. On the suffragists' attitudes toward the political parties, see Dadourian, "History of the Year, 1919–1920," NAWSA Records, cont. 51. The joint committee was discussed at a CWSA EBM, Jan. 16, 1918, NAWSA Records, cont. 51.

56. Chafe, *American Woman*, pp. 112–132; O'Neill, *Everyone Was Brave*, pp. 264–294.

57. *BH*, Nov. 14, 1920, p. 19.

Chapter Two

1. "Hearings . . . on Woman Suffrage," April 4, 1917, Katharine H. Hepburn, speaker, p. 103, and Valeria H. Parker, speaker, pp. 29–30.

2. Ruutz-Rees explained the Association's strategy in remarks before the NAWSA: to "educat[e] the public until the demand for the enfranchisement of women becomes so strong as to be irresistible." See *HWS*, V, p. 464.

3. Dadourian, interview, June 30, 1980, pp. 10, 14–15.

4. Edna Mary Purtell, interview, July 8, 1980, transcript at University of Connecticut, Storrs, pp. 53 and 17.

5. *Ibid.*, pp. 21–22.

6. *Ibid.*, p. 17.

7. In August, 1916, Pierson wrote to Windham County organizer, Rosamond Danielson, requesting that someone "pay the expenses and . . . reimburse . . . for the lost time working girls who wished to demonstrate in suffrage parades." Pierson had been asked for financial assistance by Abbie O'Connor, president of the State Self-Supporting Woman's League, who noted, "I have been always willing to make a sacrifice to help the cause." Emily Pierson to Rosamond Danielson, Aug. 12, 1916, and Abbie O'Connor to Miss Danielson, Aug. 28, 1916, NAWSA Records, cont. 52. Katherine Day provided funds for Minnie Hennesy, a shop girl who picketed and served a prison term in Washington: Katherine Day to Alice Paul, Oct. 1, 1917, Nov. 22, 1917, and Nov. 28, 1917, NWP Papers, tray 14; and Catherine Flanagan to Annie Porritt, Nov. 19, 1917, NWP Papers, tray 14.

On collecting petitions, see Anderson, *From Yankee to American*, pp. 90–93; also reports of such efforts are contained in the CWSA Papers, NAWSA Records, and NWP Papers.

An example of a pro-suffrage resolution is in "Hearings . . . on the Judiciary," 1917, pp. 140–141.

8. CWSA EBM, Oct. 9, 1918, July 17, 1918, NAWSA Records, cont. 51; Florence

Ledyard Cross Kitchelt to Rosamond Danielson, May 24, 1918, NAWSA Records, cont. 51; CWSA EBM, May 15, 1918, CWSA Papers.

9. Janick, "An Instructive Failure," p. 13; Leonard, *Woman's Who's Who*, p. 461; see also Papers of Florence Ledyard Cross Kitchelt, folders 13, 14, 15, 16, 166, Schlesinger Library, Radcliffe College; Richard Kitchelt, "Final Report," Kitchelt Papers, folder 15; CWSA EBM, Nov. 13, 1918 and Oct. 9, 1918, NAWSA Records, cont. 51; *BH*, Sept. 18, 1918, p. 3; *Hartford Courant*, Sept. 5, 1918, p. 2.

10. *BH*, Sept. 8, 1918, p. 16; "Miss Rowe's Reports, Week Ending Sept. 7th and Sept. 7th to 13th" (1918), NWP Papers, tray 17. (NWP workers Rowe, Ascough, Hill, and Todd spoke in New London and Bridgeport in Sept., 1918. *Ibid.*)

11. Alexander M. Bing, *War-Time Strikes and Their Adjustment* (New York, 1921), pp. 67-75; *BH*, Aug. and Sept., 1918; David Montgomery, "The 'New Unionism' and the Transformation of Workers' Consciousness in America, 1909-1922," *Journal of Social History*, 7 (Summer, 1974), 509-529; Montgomery, "Whose Standards? Workers and the Reorganization of Production in the United States, 1900-1920," in *Workers' Control in America* (Cambridge, England, 1979), pp. 127-134.

12. *NYT*, Aug. 15, 1915, section IV, p. 18; Hewes, *Women As Munitions Makers;* Norton, "Women in War Industries"; F. Strother, "America, A New World Arsenal: Bridgeport, Connecticut, an Example of the Effects of War Orders in the United States," *World's Work*, 31 (Jan., 1916), 321-333.

13. "Miss Rowe's Reports" (1918), NWP Papers, tray 17. Clara Peck, *BH*, Sept. 22, 1918, p. 6.

14. *Bridgeport Post*, Jan. 5, 1919; *BH*, Jan. 19, 1919, pp. 15 and 19. *BH*, Jan. 12, 1919, p. 15.

15. Katherine Day to Alice Paul, Jan. 14, 1919, and Josephine B. Bennett to Alice Paul, Jan. 16, 1919, NWP Papers, tray 20.

16. *BH*, Jan. 19, 1919, p. 1; *Bridgeport Times*, Jan. 20, 1919, p. 3.

17. Suggesting that suffragists had left-wing sympathies was a common practice of the antis; see, for example, "Hearings . . . on Woman Suffrage," 1919, pp. 9-14. In Connecticut, the charge was made more frequently against the NWP. Clearly, the association of suffragism with IAM activities in Bridgeport added fuel to the antis' arguments. CWSA EBM, Mar. 16, 1918, CWSA Papers.

18. NAWSA Records, cont. 5.

19. *Ibid.*

20. Col. Isaac Ullman, "Hearings Before His Excellancy, Marcus H. Holcomb, Governor of Connecticut," Executive Chambers, State Capitol, Hartford, March 30, 1920, NWP papers, tray 23.

21. *Ibid;* see also Dadourian, "History of the Year, 1919-1920," NAWSA Records, cont. 51.

22. Grimes, *Puritan Ethic*, p. 118; Kraditor, *Ideas*, p. 44; Chafe, *American Woman*, p. 15; O'Neill, *Everyone Was Brave*, pp. 7-75; Degler, *At Odds*, pp. 334-335.

23. CWSA, "The Republican Machine," NAWSA Records, cont. 51.

24. CWSA EBM, Jan. 22, 1919, CWSA Papers; CWSA Committee on Social Legislation, Meeting, Feb. 18, 1919, CWSA Papers.

25. "The Republican Machine," NAWSA Records, cont. 51.

26. *Ibid.*

27. Nancy Schoonmaker, CWSA EBM, Jan. 22, 1919, and EBM, Feb. 19, 1918, CWSA Papers; League of Women Voters *Bulletin*, vol. I, no. 1, published occasionally by the NAWSA, Spring, 1919, at Connecticut State Library, Hartford.

28. CWSA EBM, Oct. 9, 1918, and CWSA "Election Policy," Oct. 30, 1918, NAWSA Records, cont. 51.

29. Anne Martin to Katherine Mullen, Jan. 22, 1918, and Lillian Ascough to Anne Martin, Feb. 14, 1918, NWP Papers, tray 17; CWSA EBM, May 15, 1918, CWSA Papers; *Bridgeport Times*, Jan. 22, 1918, p. 2; Flexner, *Century of Struggle*, p. 314; "History of the Year," NAWSA Records.

30. "History of the Year;" *HWS,* VI, pp. 74–82; Alice Paul to Josephine Bennett, July 12, 1919, and Katharine H. Hepburn to Alice Paul, Feb. 27, 1920, NWP Papers, tray 23; CWSA EBM, Nov. 13, 1918, NAWSA Records, cont. 51; *HWS,* IV, p. 536.
31. *HWS,* VI, pp. 74–82; "History of the Year."
32. CWSA EBM, "Statement of Political Policy," (n.d.), NAWSA Records, cont. 51.
33. *Ibid.*
34. "History of the Year;" "Hearing . . . Before Holcomb," pp. 4–5.
35. "History of the Year."
36. Helena Hill Weed, "Confidential Report," March 11, 1920, CWSA Papers, in Herbert F. Janick, "Senator Frank B. Brandegee and the Election of 1920," *The Historian,* 35 (May, 1973), p. 442; "History of the Year."
37. "History of the Year."
38. Chafe, *American Woman,* pp. 29–30.
39. "History of the Year."
40. "Statement of Republican Suffragists," 1920, NAWSA Records, cont. 51.
41. Flexner, *Century of Struggle,* pp. 319–324.
42. *HWS,* VI, pp. 81–82.
43. *Ibid.*
44. "History of the Year."
45. *Ibid.*

Chapter Three

1. "Suffrage Songs and Verses," *The Forerunner* (New York, 1911), Connecticut State Library.
2. CWSA, "Workers' Meeting," Sept. 2, 1920, and "Business Meeting of Delegates and Workers," Sept. 24, 1920, CWSA Papers; *Republican Bulletin,* vol. 1, nos. 1 and 2, Jan. and Feb., 1922, Connecticut State Library. A statistical analysis of registration and voting patterns, while beyond the scope of this study, may provide further data on women's participation in politics in the post-suffrage era.
3. "Workers' Meeting," Sept. 2, 1920.
4. *Ibid.*
5. *Ibid.*
6. *Ibid.*
7. Support for this action was not universal among CWSA activists. Corinne Robinson Alsop announced to the meeting that she intended to vote for Brandegee. A relative newcomer to suffragism and a loyal Republican (she was the niece of Theodore Roosevelt), Alsop believed in working through the established party machinery. Her refusal to participate in the anti-Brandegee campaign did not imply support for Roraback or machine rule, however. Even as a Republican legislator (elected in 1924, 1928, and 1930), she was known for her independence. See Howes, *American Women, 1939–1940,* p. 17, and Dadourian interview, June 30, 1980, p. 30. Also on the campaign, see *BH,* Oct. 31, 1920, p. 18, October 24, 1920, p. 18, and Nov. 7, 1920, p. 7; Janick, "Brandegee," pp. 434–451.
8. Janick, "Brandegee," p. 446; "History of the Year," NAWSA Records; "Business Meeting," CWSA Papers; *BH,* Dec. 5, 1920, p. 19, Dec. 19, 1920, p. 9, Oct. 20, 1920, p. 17, Oct. 24, 1920, p. 18, Oct. 31, 1920, p. 18. CWSA, "Brandegee" File, CWSA Papers; Annie G. Porritt, "Senator Frank B. Brandegee," pp. 1–5, CWSA Papers.
9. *BH,* Oct. 24, 1920, p. 17; see also Janick, "Brandegee."
10. *BH,* Oct. 24, 1920, p. 17; Janick, "Brandegee," p. 450; "History of the Year"; Dadourian, interview, June 30, 1980, p. 26; Brandegee committed suicide in 1924; *BH,* Oct. 19, 1924, p. 37.
11. "Workers' Meeting," CWSA Papers; *Bridgeport Sunday Post,* Dec. 3, 1939, in possession of Ruth M. Dadourian, *BH,* Jan. 19, 1921, p. 1; *Hartford Courant,* Jan. 1, 1921; *Hartford Daily Times,* Jan. 20, 1927, p. 1, in possession of Ruth M. Dadourian.

12. *Ibid.*

13. *Hartford Women,* 1921 and 1922, Papers of the Hartford Woman's Club, 1896-1923, Connecticut State Library, Hartford; Papers of the Connecticut League of Women Voters (hereafter CLWV), Connecticut State Library, Hartford; *The Hartford Times,* Dec. 2, 1946, in possession of Ruth M. Dadourian; see also interviews with Marian Yeaw Biglow, June 16, 1980, Ruth McIntire Dadourian, June 30, 1980, Percy Maxim Lee, July 14, 1980, and Edith Valet Cook, Jan. 4, 1982, transcripts at University of Connecticut, Storrs.

14. See, for example, Mitchell, "Social Legislation," pp 150-158; *BH,* Jan. 7, 1923, and Feb. 11, 1923, p. 19.

15. Cook's mother was a suffragist. Cook, interview, Jan. 4, 1982; Laura Belle Reed McCoy, interview, July 30, 1980, and Celia Duhan Rostow, interview, July 16, 1980, transcripts at University of Connecticut, Storrs.

16. Josephine B. Bennett to Executive Board of the CWSA, Aug. 31, 1917, NAWSA Records, cont. 51; CLWV, *The Woman Voter's Bulletin,* vols., 6, 7 and 12, Connecticut State Library; Janick, "An Instructive Failure," pp. 12-22; *Bridgeport Sunday Post,* Dec. 3, 1939, in possession of R. M. Dadourian; "Women Voters Conduct Armament Reduction Campaign," *Hartford Women,* Jan. 6, 1922, Hartford Woman's Club Papers; Margaret Nordhoff Morrison noted in an interview, March 26, 1981, pp. 44-46, that she became involved in the peace movement through the CLWV: transcript at University of Connecticut, Storrs.

17. *Stamford Advocate,* March 29, 1939, p. 1; the *New York Times,* April 7, 1940, in possession of Emma Potter.

18. *BH,* Nov. 14, 1920, p. 19; Lee, interview, July 14, 1980, pp. 9, 11-12; Percy Maxim Lee and John Glessner Lee, *Family Reunion* (Hartford, 1971), pp. 41-45.

19. *New York Times,* March 3, 1953, p. 29, and March 21, 1953, p. 16; Biglow, interview, June 16, 1980, pp. 28 and 35; Dadourian, interview, June 30, 1980, pp. 17-18 and 28-29; Lee, interview, July 14, 1980, pp. 23-24; Howes, *American Women, 1939-1940,* p. 543.

20. *Bibliographical Cyclopaedia of American Women,* pp. 180-181; Howes, *American Women, 1939-1940.* p. 783; *Women Voter's Bulletin,* vol. 6 (July-Aug., 1926); Ruutz-Rees' willingness to allow the house to be used for a birth control center is discussed by Nancy Carnegie Rockefeller, interview, Feb. 1, 1981, p. 14; *Greenwich Times.*

21. Howes, *American Women, 1939-1940,* p. 810; Feinberg, "Grace Gallatin Seton," Sicherman and Green, *Notable American Women: The Modern Period,* pp. 639-641 (according to Feinberg, the Biblioteca Femina was donated to Northwestern University).

22. *BH,* Dec. 24, 1922, p. 19, and Dec. 31, 1922, p. 19; *Hartford Times,* Jan., 1971, in possession of Herbert Janick; Stephanie F. Ogle, "Anna Louise Strong," Sicherman and Green, *Notable American Women: The Modern Period,* pp. 664-666.

23. *Women Voter's Bulletin,* vol. 12 (1932); *BH,* Nov. 26, 1922, p. 19; "Hearings . . . on Humane Institutions," 1919, and "Hearings . . . on Labor," 1921; *Hartford Women,* Dec. 30, 1921, pp. 1 and 13.

24. Hilda Crosby Standish, interview, July 28, 1980, pp. 28-33; Rockefeller, interview, Feb. 1, 1981, p. 14; *New York Times,* March 18, 1951, p. 90; Garraty, *Dictionary of American Biography,* p. 297; Van Why, *Nook Farm,* p. 67.

25. *BH,* Dec. 19, 1920, p. 8; Purtell, interview, July 8, 1980, p. 44.

26. *BH,* Nov. 14, 1920, p. 9, Dec. 19, 1920, p. 8, Jan. 9, 1921, p. 9; *Bridgeport Sunday Post,* Dec. 3, 1939, in possession of R. M. Dadourian; Dadourian, interview, June 30, 1980, p. 27. Mitchell, "Social Legislation," pp. 157-177. The LWV was included on the list of women's organizations considered part of the socialist-pacifist movement. The "Spider Web" chart was prepared within the United States War Department in 1923; see Judith Papachristou, *Women Together* (New York, 1976), pp. 198-199; Lemons, *Woman Citizen,* pp. 214-216.

27. "Hearings . . . on Labor," 1921, 1923, 1925; "Hearings . . . on Humane Institutions," 1921, 1923; *BH,* Nov. 14, 1920, p. 19, Feb. 11, 1923, p. 19, Jan. 7, 1923, p. 19; Lemons, *Woman Citizen,* pp. 170-171; Card file of legislation proposed to Connecticut

General Assembly, 1920-1925, Connecticut State Library; *Hartford Women,* Jan. 6, 1922; Dadourian, interview, June 30, 1980, pp. 32 and 38; Mary Bulkley, *Woman Voter's Bulletin,* vol. 6, (Dec., 1926).

28. Biglow, interview, June 16, 1980, pp. 15-16.

29. CLWV, *Connecticut Voter* (Nov.-Dec., 1979), p. 4; Grasso is quoted in *Great Women of Connecticut,* State of Connecticut, Permanent Commission on the Status of Women- (Hartford, 1978), p. 23; Rita Mae Kelly and Mary Boutilier, *The Making of Political Women* (Chicago, 1978), pp. 119-121.

30. *BH,* Dec. 10, 1922, p. 19, Dec. 24, 1922, p. 19.

31. *BH,* Dec. 24, 1922, p. 19.

32. O'Neill, *Woman Movement,* pp. 92 and 63; Chafe, *American Woman,* p. 112.

33. "Hearings . . . on Labor," Feb. 23, 1923; Card file of legislation proposed to Connecticut General Assembly, 1923.

34. Chafe, *American Woman,* p. 29.

35. *Register and Manual,* 1921, pp. 509-519; *BH,* Oct. 24, 1920, p. 19.

36. *Register and Manual,* 1923, pp. 478-487, and 1925, pp. 500-509; *BH,* Oct. 15, 1922, p. 19, Oct. 29, 1922, p. 19, Nov. 12, 1922, p. 19; "Connecticut Women Holding Legislative or Official State Positions," 1921-1931, compiled by Connecticut State Library, 1931, Connecticut State Library, Hartford.

37. *BH,* Jan. 9, 1921, p. 18; Card file of legislation proposed to Connecticut General Assembly, 1921.

38. *BH,* Oct. 15, 1922, p. 19, Oct. 29, 1922, p. 19.

39. Weaver, *BH,* Nov. 12, 1922, p. 19; Brown, *BH,* Feb. 4, 1923; Emily Sophie Brown, interview, July 1, 1980, transcript at University of Connecticut, Storrs.

40. *BH,* Oct. 24, 1920, p. 17, Oct. 15, 1922, p. 13, Nov. 14, 1920, p. 19, Oct. 31, 1920, p. 19; *Register and Manual,* 1922, p. 501, 1923, pp. 478-487; on Red Scare in Connecticut, Van Dusen, *Connecticut,* pp. 277-279.

41. Cook, interview, Jan. 4, 1982, pp. 11 and 13; see also Josephine Bryant, interview, July 18, 1980, and Helen A. Green, interview, June 23, 1980, transcripts at University of Connecticut, Storrs.

42. Green, interview, June 23, 1980, pp. 11-13 and 15.

43. *New York Times,* April 7, 1940, in possession of Emma Potter.

44. Mitchell, "Social Legislation," pp. 39-42 and 67.

45. *Ibid.,* pp. 92, 125, 139.

46. Joan M. Jensen, "All Pink Sisters: The War Department and the Feminist Movement in the 1920s," in *Decades of Discontent: The Woman's Movement, 1920-1940* (Westport, 1983).

Bibliography

PRIMARY SOURCES

Manuscript Collections

Bridgeport Public Library:
   Papers of Ella G. Fleck, 1916–1931.
Connecticut State Library:
   Papers of the Connecticut League of Women Voters, 1926–1956.
   Papers of the Connecticut Peace Society, 1910–1921.
   Papers of the Connecticut Woman Suffrage Association, 1869–1921.
   Papers of the Connecticut State Council of Defense, Woman's Division.
   Papers of the Hartford Woman's Club, 1896–1923.
   Records of the Hartford Equal Franchise League, 1885–1919.
Library of Congress:
   Papers of the National Woman's Party, 1913–1920.
   Records of the National American Woman Suffrage Association.
New Haven:
   Papers of the Planned Parenthood League of Connecticut, Inc.
Schlesinger Library, Radcliffe College:
   Papers of Florence Ledyard Cross Kitchelt.

Government Documents

Connecticut General Assembly. "Public Hearings Before the Joint Standing Committee on Humane Institutions," 1917, 1919, 1921, 1923.
—————. "Public Hearings Before the Joint Standing Committee on the Judiciary," 1917.
—————. "Public Hearings Before the Joint Standing Committee on Labor," 1917, 1919, 1921, 1923, 1925.
—————. "Public Hearings Before the Joint Standing Committee on Woman Suffrage," 1915, 1917, 1919.
Connecticut Register and Manual. Hartford: State of Connecticut.
Connecticut Federation of Labor. *Official Proceedings of the Thirty-Second Annual Convention.* Danbury, September 4–7, 1917.
—————. *Official Proceedings of the Thirty-Fourth Annual Convention.* Meriden, June 2–5, 1919.
—————. *Official Proceedings of the Thirty-Fifth Annual Convention.* Waterbury, May 24–27, 1920.
—————. *Official Proceedings of the Thirty-Sixth Annual Convention.* Bridgeport, June 6–9, 1921.
Permanent Commission on the Status of Women, State of Connecticut. *Great Women of Connecticut.* Hartford, 1978.

Newspapers

Bridgeport Herald. 1917–1929.
Bridgeport Post. July, 1917; January, 1919; December, 1939.
Bridgeport Times. January, 1919.
Greenwich Time. April, 1982.

Hartford Courant. August, 1918; September, 1918; January, 1921.
Hartford Times. January, 1927; December, 1946; January, 1971.
New York Times. August 15, 1915; January 16, 1916; April 7, 1940; March 18, 1951; March 9, 1953; March 21, 1953.
Stamford *Advocate.* March 29, 1939.

Pamphlets and Miscellaneous Documents in Connecticut State Library

Connecticut League of Women Voters. *The Woman Voter's Bulletin,* VI (July-August, October, December, 1926), VII (December, 1927), and XII (September, 1932).
Connecticut State Library. "Connecticut Women Holding Legislative or Official State Positions, 1921-1931," March 23, 1931.
Charlotte Perkins Gilman. "Suffrage Songs and Verses." *The Forerunner.* New York, 1911.
Kelley, Florence. "Twenty Questions About the Proposed Equal Rights Amendment of the Woman's Party, 1923-1924." Consumers' League Pamphlet.
National American Woman Suffrage Association. *Headquarters News Letter,* II and III (January, 1916-January, 1917).
——. *League of Women Voters Bulletin,* I (April, 1919).
National League of Women Voters. "The Achievement of Ten Years" (reproductions from charts exhibited at the Tenth Anniversary Convention, 1930).
National Woman's Party. "The National Woman's Party: What It Is - What It Has Done - What It Is Doing." Washington: National Woman's Party Headquarters, no date.
Republican Bulletin, I (January and February, 1922).
Women's Republican State Central Committee of Connecticut. *Handbook of Information for Connecticut Republican Women,* 1922.

Interviews

"The Political Activities of the First Generation of Fully Enfranchised Connecticut Women: 1915-1945." Twenty-one interviews with Connecticut activists conducted by Joyce Pendery and Carole Nichols between 1980 and 1982. Transcripts located at Connecticut Humanities Resource Center, New Haven, Connecticut State Library, Hartford, and University of Connecticut, Storrs.

Radio Programs

"The Suffragists," "The League of Women Voters," "The Legislators," "The Birth Control Movement," and "Two Connecticut Women: Eleanor Little and Celia Rostow." Scripts by Carole Nichols, Joyce Pendery, and Ellen Kraft. Produced by Ellen Kraft for Connecticut Public Radio. Tapes located at Connecticut Humanities Resource Center, New Haven.

SECONDARY SOURCES

Books

Anderson, Ruth O. M. *From Yankee to American: Conecticut, 1865-1914.* Chester, CT, 1975.
Banner, Lois. *Women in Modern America.* New York, 1974.

Becker, Susan D. *The Origins of the Equal Rights Amendment: American Feminism Between the Wars.* Westport, 1981.
Berkin, Carol Ruth, and Mary Beth Norton. *Women of America: A History:* Boston, 1979.
Bing, Alexander M. *War-Time Strikes and Their Adjustment.* New York, 1921.
The Biographical Cyclopaedia of American Women. New York, 1924.
Blatch, Harriet Stanton. *Mobilizing Woman Power.* New York, 1918.
Campbell, Barbara Kuhn. *The "Liberated" Woman of 1914: Prominent Women in the Progressive Era.* Ann Arbor, 1979.
Catt, Carrie Chapman, and Nettie Rogers Shuler. *Woman Suffrage and Politics.* New York, 1923.
Chafe, William Henry. *The American Woman.* London, 1972.
Chambers, Clarke A. *Seedtime of Reform: American Social Service and Social Action, 1918–1933.* Minneapolis, 1963.
Degler, Carl. *At Odds: Women and the Family in America from the Revolution to the Present.* New York, 1980.
———. "Revolution Without Ideology." *The Woman in America.* Edited by Robert J. Lifton. Boston, 1965.
Diamond, Irene. *Sex Roles in the State House.* New Haven, 1977.
DuBois, Ellen Carol. *Feminism and Suffrage.* Ithaca, 1978.
Flexner, Eleanor. *Century of Struggle.* New York, 1959.
French, Earl A., and Diana Royce, eds. *Portraits of a Nineteenth Century Family.* Hartford, 1976.
Garraty, John A., ed. *Dictionary of American Biography.* Supplement Five, 1951–1955. New York, 1977.
Gluck, Sherna, ed. *From Parlor to Prison.* New York, 1976.
Grimes, Alan P. *The Puritan Ethic and Woman Suffrage.* New York, 1967.
Hewes, Amy. *Women As Munitions Makers.* New York, 1917.
Howes, Durward, ed. *American Women: The Standard Biographical Dictionary of Notable Women.* Three volumes. Los Angeles, 1935–1939.
Irwin, Inez Haynes. *Angels and Amazons.* Garden City, 1923.
———. *The Story of the Woman's Party.* New York, 1921.
James, Edward T., ed. *Notable American Women, 1607–1950.* Three volumes. Cambridge, MA, 1971.
Janick, Herbert F., Jr. *A Diverse People: Connecticut, 1914 to the Present.* Chester, CT, 1975.
Jensen, Joan M., and Lois Scharf. *Decades of Discontent: The Woman's Movement, 1920–1940.* Westport, 1983.
Kelly, Rita Mae, and Mary Boutilier. *The Making of Political Women.* Chicago, 1978.
Kraditor, Aileen S. *The Ideas of the Woman Suffrage Movement, 1890–1920.* Garden City, 1965.
———. *Up From the Pedestal.* New York, 1968.
Lee, John Glessner, and Percy Maxim Lee. *Family Reunion.* Hartford, 1971.
Lemons, J. Stanley. *The Woman Citizen.* Urbana, 1973.
Leonard, John William, ed. *Woman's Who's Who of America, 1914–1915.* New York, 1914.
Lerner, Gerda. *The Majority Finds Its Past.* New York, 1979.
Montgomery, David. *Workers' Control in America.* Cambridge, Eng., 1979.
Morgan, David. *Suffragists and Democrats.* East Lansing, 1972.
O'Neill, William. *Everyone Was Brave.* New York, 1971.
———. *The Woman Movement.* Chicago, 1971.
Papachristou, Judith. *Women Together.* New York, 1976.
Park, Maud Wood. *Front Door Lobby.* Boston, 1960.
Paulson, Ross Evans. *Women's Suffrage and Prohibition: A Comparative Study of Equality and Social Control.* Glenview, IL, 1973.
Roth, David M. *Connecticut.* New York, 1979.

Scharf, Lois. *To Work and to Wed: Female Employment, Feminism, and the Great Depression.* Westport, 1980.
Scott, Anne F., and Andrew M. Scott. *One Half the People: The Fight for Woman Suffrage.* Philadelphia, 1975.
Sicherman, Barbara, and Carol Hurd Green, eds. *Notable American Women: The Modern Period.* Cambridge, MA, 1980.
Sinclair, Andrew. *The Better Half: The Emancipation of the American Woman.* New York, 1965.
Stanton, Elizabeth Cady, Matilda J. Gage, Ida H. Harper, and Susan B. Anthony, eds. *History of Woman Suffrage.* Six volumes. New York, 1886–1922.
Stevens, Doris. *Jailed For Freedom.* New York, 1976.
Trecker, Janice Law. *Preachers, Rebels, and Traders: Connecticut, 1818–1865.* Chester, CT, 1975.
Van Dusen, Albert E. *Connecticut.* New York, 1961.
Van Why, Joseph S. *Nook Farm.* Hartford, 1975.
Ware, Susan. *Beyond Suffrage: Women in the New Deal.* Cambridge, MA, 1981.
Wiebe, Robert H. *The Search for Order, 1877–1920.* New York, 1967.
Wilson, Lynn Winfield. *History of Fairfield County Connecticut, 1639–1928.* Chicago-Hartford, 1929.

Articles

Conway, Jill. "Women Reformers and American Culture, 1870–1930." *Journal of Social History,* 5, no. 2 (Winter, 1971–1972), 164–178.
DuBois, Ellen. "The Radicalism of the Woman Suffrage Movement: Notes Toward the Reconstruction of Nineteenth Century Feminism." *Feminist Studies,* 3 (1975), 63–71.
Heath, Frederick M. "Labor and the Progressive Movement in Connecticut." *Labor History,* 12, no. 1 (Winter, 1971), 52–67.
Janick, Herbert F., Jr. "An Instructive Failure: The Connecticut Peace Movement, 1919–1939." *Peace and Change,* 5 (Spring, 1978), 12–22.
———. "Senator Frank B. Brandegee and the Election of 1920." *The Historian,* 35 (May, 1973), 434–451.
Jensen, Joan M. "'Disfranchisement is a Disgrace': Women and Politics in New Mexico, 1900–1940." *New Mexico Historical Review,* 56, no. 1 (January, 1981), 5–35.
Koenig, Samuel. "Ethnic Factors in the Economic Life of Urban Connecticut." *American Sociological Review,* 7, no. 2 (April, 1943), 193–197.
Lancaster, Lane W. "Background of a State Boss System." *American Journal of Sociology,* 35 (1930), 783–798.
———. "The Democratic Party in Connecticut." *National Municipal Review,* 17 (August, 1928), 451–455.
———. "Rotten Boroughs and the Connecticut Legislature." *National Municipal Review,* 13 (December, 1924), 678–683.
Montgomery, David. "The 'New Unionism' and the Transformation of Workers' Consciousness in America, 1909–1922." *Journal of Social History,* 7 (Summer, 1974), 509–529.
Norton, Esther. "Women in War Industries." *The New Republic,* December 15, 1917, pp. 179–182.
Potter, Zenas L. "War Boom Towns, Bridgeport." *The Survey,* December 4, 1915, pp. 237–242.
Strother, F. "America, A New World Arsenal: Bridgeport, Connecticut, an Example of the Effects of War Orders in the United States." *World's Work,* 31 (January, 1916), 321–333.

Unpublished Materials

Dahill, Edwin. "Connecticut's J. Henry Roraback." Unpublished Ph.D. Dissertation. Teachers College, Columbia University, 1971.
Mitchell, Rowland L., Jr. "Social Legislation in Connecticut, 1919-1939." Unpublished Ph.D. Dissertation. Yale University, 1954.
Nichols, Carole A. "A New Force in Politics: The Suffragists' Experience in Connecticut." Unpublished M.A. Thesis. Sarah Lawrence College, 1979.
Pendery, Joyce S. "Women's Secular Voluntary Organizations and Their Leaders: Stamford, Connecticut, 1860-1910." Unpublished M.A. Thesis. Sarah Lawrence College, 1978.

APPENDIX

The Leaders of the Woman Suffrage Movement in Connecticut*

NAME/ RESIDENCE	MARITAL STATUS	EDUCATION	EMPLOYMENT OTHER THAN VOLUNTEERISM	PUBLIC ACTIVITIES PRIOR TO 1920	PUBLIC ACTIVITIES AFTER 1920
Lillian Ascough Hartford	Married	Trained for concert stage in London and Paris	—	CNWP, Founder and Chairman, 1915–1918 Jailed during NWP demonstrations, 1918 and 1919	Unknown - Moved out of state, 1918
Dorothy Bartlett Putnam	Married	Unknown	—	CWSA CNWP, District Chairman Jailed during NWP demonstrations, 1917	Advocate of social legislation; speaker at legislative hearings, General Assembly Defeated candidate for state legislature, Democratic party, 1924

APPENDIX, CONTINUED

NAME/ RESIDENCE	MARITAL STATUS	EDUCATION	EMPLOYMENT OTHER THAN VOLUNTEERISM	PUBLIC ACTIVITIES PRIOR TO 1920	PUBLIC ACTIVITIES AFTER 1920
Josephine Bennett Hartford	Married	Unknown	—	DAR; Colonial Dames; Hartford anti-prostitution crusade; Hartford Equal Franchise League; CWSA, Executive Board; Treasurer, 1913–1917; War Work Committee; NWP, National Advisory Council; CNWP, Treasurer, 1917–1920; Jailed during NWP demonstrations, 1919	CLWV, organizer; Defeated candidate for U.S. Senate, Farmer-Labor party, 1920; Lived in social settlement in Katonah, NY, for a period during 1921; Defeated candidate for Attorney-General of Connecticut, Farmer-Labor party, 1922; NWP; Birth control movement
Mary Bulkley Hartford	Single	Miss Haines' School; Miss Porter's School	—	National Women's Trade Union League; Colonial Dames; World War I volunteer; Influenza epidemic volunteer; CWSA, Executive Committee, 1917–1920; Citizenship Committee; Hartford County Organizer; War Work Committee	CLWV, organizer; President, 1926–1931; Vice-President, 1934–1939; citizenship work; NLWV, National Board, Regional Director, 1930–1934; Hartford Woman's Club; Democratic party

71

APPENDIX, CONTINUED

NAME/ RESIDENCE	MARITAL STATUS	EDUCATION	EMPLOYMENT OTHER THAN VOLUNTEERISM	PUBLIC ACTIVITIES PRIOR TO 1920	PUBLIC ACTIVITIES AFTER 1920
Ruth McIntire Dadourian Hartford	Married	Buckingham School, Cambridge, MA Miss Wilkens' School, Belmont, MA BA, Radcliffe, 1912	Writer Publicist, National Child Labor Committee	Suffrage demonstrations, Cambridge, MA CWSA Executive Board, 1918–1920; Publicity and Press Work, 1918–1920; Executive Secretary, 1920	CLWV, Executive Board; Secretary; President Executive Secretary, Connecticut Commission on Child Welfare Lobbyist for social legislation, General Assembly Author, *Party Machinery: The Caucus and Convention System of Connecticut* Works Progress Administration, Supervisor, Women's Projects President, Connecticut Tuberculosis Association West Hartford Taxpayers Association, Board Member West Hartford Campaign for Council-Manager Government Board of Trustees, Connecticut Agricultural College (now Univ. of CT, Storrs)

APPENDIX, CONTINUED

NAME/ RESIDENCE	MARITAL STATUS	EDUCATION	EMPLOYMENT OTHER THAN VOLUNTEERISM	PUBLIC ACTIVITIES PRIOR TO 1920	PUBLIC ACTIVITIES AFTER 1920
Rosamond Danielson Putnam	Single	Unknown	—	World War I volunteer CWSA, Executive Board; Windham County Chairman, 1917–1920; War Work Committee	CLWV Women's Non-Partisan Committee for the League of Nations
Katherine Beach Day Hartford	Married	Unknown	—	Hartford anti-prostitution crusade Social Hygiene CWSA, Executive Board; Membership Chairman NWP, National Advisory Council CNWP, Advisory Council; Membership Chairman	CLWV, Director, organizer NWP Birth control movement
Catherine M. Flanagan Hartford	Single	Unknown	Paid suffragist	CWSA, Organizer NWP, National Organizer; Organization Secretary Worked in Jeannette Rankin's campaign for Congress, 1918, Montana Jailed during NWP demonstrations, 1917	Unknown

73

APPENDIX, CONTINUED

NAME/ RESIDENCE	MARITAL STATUS	EDUCATION	EMPLOYMENT OTHER THAN VOLUNTEERISM	PUBLIC ACTIVITIES PRIOR TO 1920	PUBLIC ACTIVITIES AFTER 1920
Ella G. Fleck Bridgeport	Married	Unknown	—	Advocate of child welfare Advocate of public health services World War I volunteer, Chairman of Bridgeport Minute Women Influenza epidemic volunteer CWSA, War Work Committee	Connecticut League of Republican Women Colored Women's Political Club of Bridgeport, helped to organize Bridgeport Appointment Board (appointed by Mayor) Advocate of public health services; elimination of child labor; and juvenile court system
Katharine Houghton Hepburn Hartford	Married	BA, Bryn Mawr, 1899 MA, Bryn Mawr, 1900	Teacher in Baltimore	Hartford anti-prostitution crusade Hartford Equal Franchise League CWSA, Executive Board 1910–1920; President, 1910–1911 and 1913–1917 NWP, National Executive Committee CNWP, Chairman, 1919–1920	CLWV, Director, organizer Birth control movement

APPENDIX, CONTINUED

NAME/ RESIDENCE	MARITAL STATUS	EDUCATION	EMPLOYMENT OTHER THAN VOLUNTEERISM	PUBLIC ACTIVITIES PRIOR TO 1920	PUBLIC ACTIVITIES AFTER 1920
Elsie Mary Hill Norwalk	Married (kept own name)	Mrs. Mead's School, Norwalk BA, Vassar, 1906 Universities of Rome and Paris Yale Law School	Teacher	DAR Vassar Alumnae Association Summer School of Philanthropy, member Association of Collegiate Alumnae Washington, D.C. Equal Suffrage League, President Norwalk Equal Franchise League CWSA, Organizer Congressional Union, Executive Committee NWP, National Organizer CNWP, District Chairman Jailed during NWP demonstrations, 1918 and 1919	Defeated candidate for Secretary of the State, Farmer-Labor party, 1920 NWP, National Chairman, 1921–1925; National Council Defeated candidate for state legislature, Independent Republican party. 1928. Defeated candidate for U.S. Congress, Independent Republican party, 1932 AAUW Redding Civic League

APPENDIX, CONTINUED

NAME/ RESIDENCE	MARITAL STATUS	EDUCATION	EMPLOYMENT OTHER THAN VOLUNTEERISM	PUBLIC ACTIVITIES PRIOR TO 1920	PUBLIC ACTIVITIES AFTER 1920
Maud M. Hincks Bridgeport	Married	Vassar	—	Visiting Nurses Association YWCA Pure Milk for Babies Association Bridgeport Hospital volunteer World War I volunteer; Chairman, Liberty Loan Committee; Connecticut State Council for Defense CWSA, President, 1911–1913; Executive Board	Women's Non-Partisan Committee for the League of Nations
Florence Ledyard Cross Kitchelt New London	Married	BA, Wells College, 1897 New York School for Philanthropy	Social worker, settlement houses in NY Paid suffragist Author	Consumer's League Socialist party Worker for trade unionism Political Equality Club CWSA, Windham County Organizer	CLWV, Citizenship Education Author, works on criminal justice Campaign for LaFollette, 1924 Connecticut League of Nations Association, Executive Director, 1924–1944 Connecticut Committee for the Equal Rights Amendment, 1943–1956

APPENDIX, CONTINUED

NAME/RESIDENCE	MARITAL STATUS	EDUCATION	EMPLOYMENT OTHER THAN VOLUNTEERISM	PUBLIC ACTIVITIES PRIOR TO 1920	PUBLIC ACTIVITIES AFTER 1920
Katharine Ludington Old Lyme	Single	Miss Porter's School Travel abroad	Portrait painter	World War I volunteer CWSA, Executive Board; New London County Chairman; Chairman, War Work Committee; President, 1917-1920	NLWV, founder; Regional Director; Vice-President; Treasurer CLWV, Executive Board; President Connecticut College for Women, Trustee United Nations Association
Josephine Hamilton Maxim Hartford	Married	Mlle. Charbonnier's French School, New York	—	Colonial Dames Hartford Garden Club CWSA, Executive Board; Corresponding Secretary; Political Leader	CLWV, Vice-President Hartford LWV, President Delegate (alternate) to Democratic National Convention, 1920 Defeated candidate for state senate, Democratic party, 1920 Hartford Democratic Town Committee, Vice-Chairman Democratic State Central Committee, Women's Auxiliary Delegate-at-large, "Repeal" Convention, 1933 Hartford Public Welfare Commission Hartford Board of Health Hartford Board of Education

APPENDIX, CONTINUED

NAME/ RESIDENCE	MARITAL STATUS	EDUCATION	EMPLOYMENT OTHER THAN VOLUNTEERISM	PUBLIC ACTIVITIES PRIOR TO 1920	PUBLIC ACTIVITIES AFTER 1920
Kate Campbell Hurd Mead Middletown	Married	MD, Women's Medical College of PA, 1888 Johns Hopkins Medical School	Gynecologist	Advocate of public health services; milk stations for babies; nursing services World War I volunteer; Connecticut State Council of Defense CWSA	CLWV Women's Non-Partisan Committee for the League of Nations Visiting Nurses Association Public Health International Association of Medical Women, National Secretary, 1929-1939 Author, works on history of women in medicine
Katherine Mullen New Haven	Single	Teacher training	Teacher Paid suffragist	World War I volunteer CWSA, New Haven County Organizer NWP, National Organizer CNWP, Organizer Worked in Anne Martin's campaign for U.S. Senate in Nevada, 1918	Unknown

APPENDIX, CONTINUED

NAME/ RESIDENCE	MARITAL STATUS	EDUCATION	EMPLOYMENT OTHER THAN VOLUNTEERISM	PUBLIC ACTIVITIES PRIOR TO 1920	PUBLIC ACTIVITIES AFTER 1920
Valeria Hopkins Parker Greenwich	Married	BA, Oxford (Ohio) College MD, Herring Medical College, Chicago Travel abroad	Physician	Founder, Emily Bruce Children's Home Promoted health and sex education and lectured in secondary schools Social Hygiene Advocate of social welfare legislation, particularly for women and children Consumers' League World War I volunteer, Connecticut State Council of Defense Greenwich Equal Franchise League CWSA, Press Chairman CNWP, Vice-Chairman Connecticut State Farm for Women, Secretary of the Board	CLWV, organizer Advocate of social legislation; speaker at legislative hearings, General Assembly Connecticut Commission on Social Hygiene U.S. Social Hygiene Board, Executive Director Consumers' League Housewives' League

APPENDIX, CONTINUED

NAME/ RESIDENCE	MARITAL STATUS	EDUCATION	EMPLOYMENT OTHER THAN VOLUNTEERISM	PUBLIC ACTIVITIES PRIOR TO 1920	PUBLIC ACTIVITIES AFTER 1920
Emily Pierson Cromwell	Single	BA, Vassar, 1907 MA, Columbia, 1908 MD, Yale, 1924	Teacher Paid suffragist Physician	Advocate of social welfare legislation; particular concern for child welfare, education, labor problems, working conditions of women and children Social Hygiene National Collegiate Equal Franchise League Women's Political Union, NY Hartford Equal Franchise League CWSA, Organizer NWP, National Organizer CNWP, Organizer	NWP School Physician, Cromwell Director of Health, Cromwell Traveler; speaker on life in socialist countries

APPENDIX, CONTINUED

NAME/ RESIDENCE	MARITAL STATUS	EDUCATION	EMPLOYMENT OTHER THAN VOLUNTEERISM	PUBLIC ACTIVITIES PRIOR TO 1920	PUBLIC ACTIVITIES AFTER 1920
Annie G. Porritt Hartford	Married	Elmswood College, England, with high honors, Cambridge exams	Teacher Journalist Lecturer	Hartford School Board CWSA, Press Secretary, Executive Board NWP, National Advisory Council CNWP, Press Secretary; Advisory Council	CLWV, Vice-President; Secretary; citizenship education Hartford LWV NWP Birth control movement
Caroline Ruutz-Rees Greenwich	Single	LLA, St. Andrews, Scotland, 1904 MA, Columbia PhD, Columbia 1910 Yale University Study in Paris and Grenoble	Headmistress, Rosemary Hall School Author, scholarly articles on literature	World War I volunteer, National Council of Defense, State Council of Defense Greenwich Equal Franchise League CWSA, Executive Board; War Work Committee; Fairfield County Chairman NAWSA, Committee on Literature, Chairman; organized National Junior Suffrage Corps	CLWV, Executive Board NLWV, Executive Committee Women's Democratic Alliance, President, 1920 Democratic State Central Committee Democratic National Committee Women's Non-Partisan Committee for the League of Nations National Recovery Administration, Woman Chairman for Connecticut AAUW Fairfield State Hospital, Trustee Woodrow Wilson Foundation, Trustee

81

APPENDIX, CONTINUED

NAME/ RESIDENCE	MARITAL STATUS	EDUCATION	EMPLOYMENT OTHER THAN VOLUNTEERISM	PUBLIC ACTIVITIES PRIOR TO 1920	PUBLIC ACTIVITIES AFTER 1920
Nancy Musselman Schoonmaker Hartford	Married	Transylvania University, KY Sorbonne, Paris	Essayist Poet Dramatist Paid suffragist	Advocate of social welfare legislation, with particular concern for problems of women workers CWSA, Chairman of Citizenship Committee	CLWV, citizenship education Democratic party activist
Daphne Selden Hartford	Married in 1920	College graduate	Teacher Paid suffragist	World War I volunteer in France CWSA, Executive Board; Organizer	Unknown - Moved out of state, 1920
Grace Gallatin Seton Greenwich	Married	Packer Collegiate Institute, Brooklyn, NY Travel abroad	Writer Explorer Lecturer Book designer	Advocate of social welfare legislation, with particular concern for shorter work week for women Camp Fire Girls, organizer World War I volunteer in France Women's Political Union, NY Greenwich Equal Franchise League NAWSA, Director of Art Publicity CWSA, Executive Board; Vice-President; Vice-Chairman, Congressional Committee	President, National League of American Pen Women Established Biblioteca Femina Republican party activist Author of travel books with emphasis on conditions and status of women in other cultures

APPENDIX, CONTINUED

NAME/ RESIDENCE	MARITAL STATUS	EDUCATION	EMPLOYMENT OTHER THAN VOLUNTEERISM	PUBLIC ACTIVITIES PRIOR TO 1920	PUBLIC ACTIVITIES AFTER 1920
Mabel Washburn Hartford	Single	Unknown	Paid Suffragist	World War I volunteer Women's Committee, Connecticut State Council of Defense CWSA, Executive Board	CLWV, President; citizenship education
Helena Hill Weed Norwalk	Married	BA, Vassar, 1896 MA, Vassar, 1902 Montana School of Mines Travel and study abroad	Geologist Editorial work	DAR World War I volunteer Civic work, especially interested in public schools Socialist party New York Equal Franchise League Norwalk Equal Franchise League CNWP Jailed during NWP demonstrations, 1917 and 1918	Progressive party activist NWP

83

APPENDIX, CONTINUED

NAME/RESIDENCE	MARITAL STATUS	EDUCATION	EMPLOYMENT OTHER THAN VOLUNTEERISM	PUBLIC ACTIVITIES PRIOR TO 1920	PUBLIC ACTIVITIES AFTER 1920
Fannie Dixon Welch Tolland	Married	Private school in Neuilly, France	Farmer	American Red Cross World War I volunteer CWSA, Executive Board; Tolland County Chairman; War Work Committee	CLWV Connecticut Federation of Democratic Women's Clubs, President 4H Club Town Chairman Connecticut Child Welfare Association Defeated candidate for Secretary of the State, Democratic party, 1920 Justice of the Peace Democratic State Central Committee, Vice-Chairman Democratic National Committeewoman TB Commissioner Collector of Customs
Mary Crowell Welles Newington	Single	BA, Smith PhD, Yale	College professor Consumers' League (paid lobbyist)	American Association for Labor Legislation Connecticut Peace Society National Child Labor Committee CWSA	CLWV, Chairman, Women in Industry Committee Consumers' League lobbyist Defeated candidate for Connecticut legislature, Independent, 1922 and 1924

APPENDIX, CONTINUED

NAME/ RESIDENCE	MARITAL STATUS	EDUCATION	EMPLOYMENT OTHER THAN VOLUNTEERISM	PUBLIC ACTIVITIES PRIOR TO 1920	PUBLIC ACTIVITIES AFTER 1920
Josepha Whitney New Haven	Widowed in 1911	Private schools in Washington, Paris, Geneva, and Berlin	Artist	Woman's Peace Party, Chairman, Connecticut Chapter; New Haven Equal Franchise League, President; CWSA, New Haven County Chairman; War Work Committee	CLWV; New Haven LWV, President; Delegate-at-Large, Democratic National Convention, 1920; League of Nations Association; Connecticut Federation of Democratic Women's Clubs, Vice-President; Defeated candidate for Connecticut Senate, Democratic party, 1922; Legislator, Connecticut House of Representatives, Democratic party, 1933 and 1935; New Haven Board of Aldermen, 1928–1930

85

*The purpose of this chart is to highlight the range of political interests of the women who led Connecticut's suffrage movement, especially after the suffrage victory. Further research can reveal still more about their activities and numerous organizational ties throughout their lives.

Abbreviations:
- AAUW — American Association of University Women
- CLWV — Connecticut League of Women Voters
- CNWP — Connecticut Branch of the National Woman's Party
- CWSA — Connecticut Woman Suffrage Association
- DAR — Daughters of the American Revolution
- LWV — League of Women Voters
- NAWSA — National American Woman Suffrage Association
- NLWV — National League of Women Voters
- NWP — National Woman's Party
- YWCA — Young Women's Christian Association

Sources:
Papers of the Connecticut Woman Suffrage Association, the Hartford Woman's Club, and the Connecticut League of Women Voters (Connecticut State Library, Hartford); Papers of the National Woman's Party and Records of the National American Woman Suffrage Association (Library of Congress); Connecticut General Assembly, Public Hearings Before the Joint Standing Committees on Humane Institutions, on the Judiciary, on Labor, and on Woman Suffrage; *Connecticut Register and Manual* (Hartford); *Bridgeport Herald; Hartford Courant; New York Times; The Biographical Cyclopaedia of American Women* (New York, 1924); John A. Garraty, ed., *Dictionary of American Biography,* Supplement Five, 1951–1955 (New York, 1977; Durward Howes, ed., *American Women: The Standard Biographical Dictionary of Notable Women,* 3 vols. (Los Angeles, 1935–1939); Percy Maxim Lee and John Glessner Lee, *Family Reunion* (Hartford, 1971); Edward T. James, ed., *Notable American Women, 1607–1950,* 3 vols. (Cambridge, MA, 1971); Barbara Sicherman and Carol Hurd Green, eds., *Notable American Women: The Modern Period* (Cambridge, MA, 1980); John William Leonard, ed., *Woman's Who's Who of America, 1914–1915* (New York, 1914); Stanton, Elizabeth Cady, Matilda J. Gage, Ida. H. Harper, and Susan B. Anthony, eds., *History of Woman Suffrage,* 6 vols. (New York, 1886–1922).

Index

AAUW, 49
Alsop, Corinne (founder, League of Republican women), 40,50,57 n.24,62 n.7
Anthony, Susan B., 6,53 n.1
Anti-suffragists, women as, 15-16,40,45; and prohibition, 15
Ascough, Lillian, 70

Bacon, Elizabeth, 7,9-10; CWSA secretary, 9
Baldwin, Gov. Simeon E. (Dem.), 11
Bartlett, Dorothy, 70
Beecher, Catherine, 6,56 n.5
Beecher, Lyman, 6
Bennett, Josephine Beach, 8,13,18,19, 32,43,46,71; Bridgeport speech, 27; imprisoned, 27-28; Senate candidate, Farmer-Labor party, 49
Berkin, Carol Ruth, 54 n.2
Biblioteca Femina, 43. *See also* Seton, Grace Gallatin
Biglow, Marian Yeaw, 45. *See also* women as anti-suffragists; CLWV
Birth control, 43-44; laws, 41; illegal clinics, 43,63 n.20; Birth Control League, 21
Brandegee, Sen. Frank, 32,34,37-40,62 nn.7-10. *See also* Republican Party: opposition to suffragists
Bridgeport, 26-28,49,74,76; navy yard, 1918 strike at, 26; *Herald,* 27. *See also* International Association of Machinists; Lavit, Sam
Bridgeport Ladies Machinist Union, 27
Bristol, Conn., 48; High School, 13
Brown, Emily Sophie, 48-50; Republican Representative, 48; New Haven County Commissioner, 49 *See also* Politics: Women in
Brown, Rev. Olympia, 6
Bryant, Louise, 28
Bulkley, Mary, 28-29; President, CLWV, 40,45
Burns, Lucy, 18
Burr, Frances Ellen: Pioneering suffragist, 5-6

Camp Fire Girls, 13
Catt, Carrie Chapman: Introduces NAWSA "Six-Year Plan," 17
Chafe, William H., 35,46,53 n.1
Chamber of Commerce, Conn., 44
Child Labor, 2,4,9,41,44,49; proposed 1919 legislation on, 30; as concern of women legislators, 50
Child welfare, 48
Civil service system, state, 11
Cleveland, 1853 women's rights convention in, 5
CLWV (Connecticut League of Women Voters), 21,31; former suffragists join, 42-44; political education program of, 45; broadened membership of, 48-50. *See also* LWV
Colored Women's Clubs, Federation of, 44. *See also* New Haven
Columbia University, 13
Congressional Union. *See* CU
Connecticut Association Opposed to Suffrage, 15. *See also* Anti-suffragists, women as
Connecticut Child Welfare Association, 41
Connecticut Federation of Labor:

© 1983 by The Haworth Press, Inc. All rights reserved. 87

endorses 19th amendment, 26
Connecticut League of Women Voters.
  See CLWV
Connecticut Light and Power Company,
  31,57 n.25. *See also* Roraback, J.
  Henry
Connecticut Order of Women
  Legislators, 50. *See also* OWLs;
  Politics, women in
Connecticut Unemployment and Relief
  Commission, 4
Connecticut Woman Suffrage
  Association. *See* CWSA
Convention, 1869 Conn. suffrage. *See*
  Suffrage, women's: convention,
  1869
Consumers' League, 45,47,48
Cook, Edith Valet, 41; Republican
  representative, 49-50. *See also*
  Politics, women in
Corning Glass Works, 13
Corrupt practices act, 11
Corset Workers Union, 27
Council of Jewish Women. *See* Jewish
  Women, Council of
Cromwell, Conn., 43,80
Cross, Gov. Wilbur (Dem.), 3,44
CU (Congressional Union), 18. *See also*
  Paul, Alice; NWP
CWSA (Connecticut Woman Suffrage
  Association), 8,44,51,56 n.1; 58 nn.
  35-36; founded, 5-6; early influence
  of evaluated, 9-10; 1910 convention
  of, 14; post-1910 leadership of,
  13-15; and prohibition, 16; and war
  effort (WWI), 17,59 nn.42-44;
  differences with NAWSA, 18-19;
  and the NWP, 19-20, 1915-20
  activities of, 23-26; and labor,
  28-29; and 1919 General Assembly,
  30-33; Citizenship Committee of,
  31,37; and non-partisanship, 33;
  Jubilee Convention of (1919), 33;
  abandons non-partisanship, 35-40

Dadourian, Ruth McIntire, 19,72; New
  Deal official, 4; evaluates NWP,
  20; joins CWSA, 24; quoted, 3,36,
  40,44,45

Danielson, Rosamond, 73
Davis, Paulina Wright, 6
Day, Katherine Beach, 13,28,43,46;
  board member, CU and CWSA, 18
Debs, Eugene, 24
Degler, Carl: theory disputed, 7,53 n.1
Democratic Party, Conn., 4; nominates
  Annie Porritt to Hartford Board of
  Education, 8; weakness of,
  11,39,48; endorses women's
  suffrage, 11,32; supports 19th
  amendment, 33; women in, 4,38,44,
  49
Democratic National Committee, 43
Divorce, 46
Dodge, Josephine, 15. *See also* Anti-
  suffragists, women as
Douglas, Frederick 6
Dubois, Ellen Carol, 53-54 n.1
Dworkin, Mary: Workers' Party
  Nominee, 49

Eighteenth (Prohibition) Amendment, 16
Emery, Julia: forms Conn. OWLs, 50
Equal-rights leagues, 19th-century, 1,7
Equality, women's: 1869 resolution re,
  7; before the law, 46

Factory inspection. *See* Labor legislation
Family-welfare legislation. *See* Birth
  control; Reform, social
Farmer-Labor Party, 43,49
Flanagan, Catherine, 18-19; quoted, 20
Foreign-born population. *See* Immigrants

Garrison, William Lloyd, 6
Girl Scouts, 41
"Glastonbury, Maids of." *See* Smith,
  Julia and Abby
Goldin, State Sen. Eugene, 47
Granby, Conn., 49
Grasso, Ella, 46,64 n.29
Green, Helen A.: Republican General
  Assembly nominee, 49
Greenwich, Conn., 12,79,81-82;
  Committee for Maternal Health, 43
Guilford, Conn., 4

Handicapped, aid for, 45

Index

Hartford, 12,13,20,24,42,70-74,77, 81-83; Board of Education, 8; *Courant,* 12,44; prostitution in, 13; Political Equality League (later Equal Franchise League), 14; Maternal Health Center, 43
Hepburn, Dr. Thomas N., 13,43
Hepburn, Katharine Houghton, 12,24,32, 74; and social hygiene, 13,58 n.32; elected president CWSA 14; and NWP, 18-20; and birth control, 43-44
Hill, Elsie Mary, 19,46,75; on CU executive committee, 18; as NWP activist, 26-27; as political candidate, 49
Holcomb, Gov. Marcus, 29,32-36. *See also* Republican Party: and opposition to suffragists
Holt, Viola, State Sen., 48
Hooker, Isabella Beecher, 56 n.4; leads call for 1869 suffrage convention, 6; dominates CWSA, 10
Hooker, John, 6
Hooker, Rep. Mary, 48
Howe, Julia Ward, 6
Howell, Mrs. Richard, 25

IAM (International Association of Machinists), 26-28. *See also* Labor, cooperation with
Immigrants, 10-11
Imprisonment of women activists, 18-19, 27-28,59 nn.47-49,60 n.7
International Association of Machinists. *See* IAM

Jensen, Joan M., 51
Jewell, Gov. Marshall and Esther, 6,15
Jewett, Helen, State Rep., 48
Jewish Women, Council of, 44
Johnston, William: IAM national president, 26
Jury duty for women, 2,4,45
Juvenile courts, 41

Kitchelt, Florence Ledyard Cross, 41,76; CWSA organizer, 25. *See also* Kitchelt, Richard

Kitchelt, Richard, 25; CWSA labor organizer, 26
Koenig, Samuel, 10
Kraditor, Aileen, 53 n.1
Krawchuk, Samuel, 28

Labor Board, United States, 26
Labor, alliances with. *See* Women's movement: labor, alliances with
Labor legislation, 2,4,9,17,30,41,45; re factory inspection, 9,50; re safety, 9; re ten-hour day, 9
Lavit, Mrs. Sam, 27
Lavit, Sam: IAM Local Agent, Bridgeport, 26,28
Law, women admitted to practice of, 9
League of Nations Associations, 43
League of Nursing, 44
League of Republican Women, 40,44
League of Women Voters. *See* LWV
League of Women Voters, Conn. *See* CLWV
Lee, Percy Maxim: President, LWV, 42
Little, Eleanor H.: Chief administrator, Conn. Unemployment and Relief Commission, 4
Lonergan, Cong. Augustin, 32,39
Long Ridge Suffrage Club, 10
Ludington, Katharine, 31,33,36,42,59 n.52,77; and war work, 17; becomes president of CWSA, 19; on joining political parties, 38
LWV (League of Women Voters), 3,19, 37,38,41; opposed, 44. *See also* Women's movement: in Post-suffrage era; CLWV

McCoy, Laura Belle Reed, 41
McLean, Mrs. George, 15
McLean, Sen, George 28-29,32,34. *See also* Republican Party: and opposition to suffrage
Machinists' Union. *See* International Association of Machinists
Manufacturers' Association of Conn., 44
Markham, Mrs. Daniel A.: Head of Conn. Assoc. Opposed to Suffrage, 15. *See also* Anti-suffragists, women as

Maternity care, 41
Maxim, Josephine Hamilton: Founder, CLWV, 42
Men's Ratification Committee (MRC). *See* Republican Men's Ratification Committee
Middletown, Conn., 78
Militancy, differences over, 18-20. *See also* Women's Movement: organizations, differences among
Mitchell, Rowland, 44,51
Mullen, Katherine, 18
Munitions factories. *See* Working women: in munitions factories
Muriel McSweeney Club, 24

NAACP, 44
National American Woman Suffrage Association. *See* NAWSA
National Association Opposed to Woman Suffrage, 15. *See also* Anti-suffragists, women as
National Child Labor Committee, 24
National Council of Women, 43
National League of American Pen Women, 43
National Recovery Administration, 43
National Woman Suffrage Association, 6. *See also* NAWSA
National Woman's Party. *See* NWP
Naugatuck, Conn., 48
NAWSA (National American Woman Suffrage Association), 6,19,32,58 n.36; Congressional Committee of, 18; "Six-Year Plan," 17-18; and nativism, 29
New Deal, 4
New England Woman Suffrage Association, 6
New Haven, 29,41,48,78,85; "colored suffrage league" in, 25
New London, 76
Newington, Conn., 84
Nineteenth Amendment, 1-2,8,18,20,24, 26,39; ratification drive, 31-36, 59-60 n.52
NLWV. *See* LWV
Norwalk, 75,83
NWP (National Woman's Party), 8,23, 24,32,44; formed, 18-19; and the CWSA, 20; and the IAM, 26-28; evaluated 46,47; Connecticut Branch of, 14,43,46. *See also* Militancy, differences over; Women's movement: organizations

O'Neill, William, 46,53 n.1,54 n.3,55 n.5
Old Lyme, Conn., 19,43,77
Order of Women Legislators (OWLs), 42,50

Packer Collegiate Institute, 13
Pankhurst, Emmeline, 13,14
Parker, Valeria Hopkins, 12,19,79; and social hygiene, 13,43
Paul, Alice, 20,28,46; of the Congressional Union (CU), 18. *See also* National Woman's Party (NWP)
Peace movement, women in, 41,48,63 n.16
Pierson, Emily, 12,13,18,46,80; trips to Soviet Union and China, 43
Police matrons, 9
Politics, women in local and state: 1,3; as members of party committees, 2; offices open to, at turn of the century, 9; as candidates, 2,8,41, 47-49; in political parties, 38; as legislators, 50,64 n.36. *See also* Democratic Party, women in; Republican Party, women in; Brandegee, Sen. Frank
Pollution, 41,49
Porritt, Annie G., 7,14,18,81; elected to Hartford Board of Education, 8; letter re CWSA, 20; and birth control, 43
Prentice, Mrs. Samuel O., 15. *See also* Anti-suffragists, women as
Progressive Era, 10,12
Prohibition, 15; Republicans opposed to, 12; suffragists and, 16
Prostitution, 41. *See also* Hartford, prostitution in
Public health, 43
Public life, women in, in 19th century, 5
Purtell, Edna Mary: imprisoned, 24-25;

Index

disagrees with LWV on nonpartisanship, 44
Putnam, Conn., 70,73

Radcliffe College, 24
Reapportionment. *See* Rural domination of government
Reform, political, 56 n.2,62 n.7; local success and statewide failure, 3; under Gov. Baldwin, 11; postsuffrage failure, 47,53 n.1
Reform, social, 2; opposition to, 3; supported by women, 3,41; 1869 resolutions re, 6-7; women's suffrage as vehicle for, 12-13, 15-16,23,53 n.1,54 n.3
Republican machine, 5,11-12,15,30,32, 56 n.2,57 n.25. *See also* Roraback, J. Henry
Republican Men's Ratification Committee, 29,33,34
Republican Party, Conn., 35; and opposition to suffrage, 3,5,10,11,32, 62 n.7; at variance with national party, 20; State Central Committee, 33,57 n.25; newspapers controlled by, 12; women in, 33,38,62 n.7. *See also* Republican machine
Republican Party, National, 33; National Committee, 43
Road improvement, 41
Rochester, N.Y., 25
Roraback, J. Henry, 11-12,31,44,50,57 n.25. *See also* Republican machine
Rosemary Hall School for Girls, 13,43
Rostow, Celia Duhan: Socialist candidate, 41
Rowe, Clara Louise, 26-27. *See also* Hill, Elsie Mary
Rural domination of government, 10,24, 51; and opposition to reappportionment, 12,57 n.20
Russell, Mrs.: opposes alliance with labor, 29
Ruutz-Rees, Caroline, 12,13,43,81; as New Deal official, 4

Sanger, Margaret, 44

School elections, women voting in, 7; school suffrage law passed 1893, 7; amended 1897, 9; decline of, explained, 7-8
Schoonmaker, Nancy Musselman: CWSA activist, 31,82
Secretary of the State of Conn., woman elected, 4
Selden, Daphne, 82
Seton, Ernest Thompson, 13
Seton, Grace Gallatin, 12-13,82,63 n.21; in World War I, 17; vice-president of CWSA, 19; establishes Biblioteca Femina, 43
Sheppard-Towner Maternity and Infancy Protection Act, 45
Smith College, 45
Smith, Julia and Abby, 7,56 n.7
Social-welfare legislation, 9,30,48; programs, 10
Soviet Union, 43
Stamford, Conn., 50
Stanton, Elizabeth Cady, 6
Stone, Lucy, 6
Stowe, Harriet Beecher, 6,56 n.5
Stratford, Conn., 25,39
Strong, Anna Louise, 43
Suffrage, women's: Resolutions of 1867, 6,7; convention, 1869, 6-7. *See also* CWSA; Democratic Party: endorses women's suffrage; Nineteenth Amendment; NAWSA; Republican Party: and opposition to suffrage; Reform, social: women's suffrage as vehicle for; Women's movement; Working women: and suffrage
Suffragists, 2; characteristics of,14-15, 23,54 n.3; and nativism, 29-30, 54-55 n.3; accused of radicalism, 15,61 n.17; as local activists, 1; post-1910 campaign activities, 14-16; and World War I (*See* CWSA and war effort). *See also* Anti-suffragists, women as; Prohibition: suffragists and; Reform, social: women's movement as vehicle for; Women's movement; Working women: and suffrage
Sweatshops, 4

Taxation, 51; resisted by "Maids of Glastonbury," 7
Temperance, 9
Tennessee ratifies 19th amendment, 35,36
Third-party candidates, women as, 41,49
Tolland, Conn., 48,84
Town caucuses, women admitted to, 38
Travelers Insurance Company, 24,25
Trinity College, 24

Ullman, Isaac, 29
United Nations, 42
United Nations Association, 19
Urbanization, 12

Van Dusen, Albert E., 11
Vassar College, 13
Vernon, Mabel, 8
Vervane Elsie: President, Bridgeport Ladies Machinist Union, 27-28
Voter registration, 37

War Work, CWSA Central Committee on, 17,59 n.42
Washburn, Mabel, 83
Washington, state of: ratifies 19th amendment, 34
Waterbury, 44
WCTU, 44
Weaver, State Rep. Mary B., 48
Weed, Helena Hill: NWP worker, 34,83
Welch, Fannie Dixon, 84
Welles, Mary Crowell: Consumers' League lobbyist, 47,84
Wellesley College, 48
Wells College, 25
Whitney, Josepha, 41; Democratic candidate, 48
Widows' pensions, 30-31,41
Willimantic, Conn., 25; 1895 school election, 8
Wilson, Woodrow, 18,26-28
Wohl, Clara: NWP activist, 28
Woman's Party. *See* National Woman's Party (NWP)
Women in Politics. *See* Politics, Women in
Women's movement: impact of, evaluated, 1; goals and purposes of, 2,4,42,45; historians on, 1,7,35,51, 52-55 nn.1-2; in late 19th century, 1,6-10; vs. male political power, 3, 8,12,38; in post-suffrage era, 1,2, 26-27,37-52,55 nn.5,14 (*see also* LWV); labor, and alliances with, 2, 26-28, leadership of, 12,55 n.12 (*See also* Hepburn, Katharine Houghton; Hill, Elsie; Ludington, Katharine; Parker, Valeria Hopkins; Pierson, Emily; Ruutz-Rees, Caroline; Seton, Grace Gallatin; and pp. 70-85); single women in, 14; tactics of, 16,18,31,37,38-40,45-46, 58 n.40; organizations, differences among, 18-20,55 n.4,59 n.49,60 n.53; organizations, national vs. state, 1,18,21 (*See also* CWSA, LWV, NWP); opposition to (*See* Republican Party, and opposition to suffrage). *See also* Politics, women in
Women's property, 31,46
Workers' party, 49
Working: conditions, 2; hours, 4,41,45
Working women: and suffrage, 15,25,54 n.3; in munitions factories, 17,59 n.44
Workman's compensation, 11

Yale University, 39; Law School, 46
Yankee dominance, 10,11